Project:

Print

An Hachette UK Company
www.hachette.co.uk

First published in the United Kingdom in 2020 by Ilex,
an imprint of Octopus Publishing Group Ltd,
Carmelite House, 50 Victoria Embankment,
London EC4Y 0DZ
www.octopusbooks.co.uk
www.octopusbooksusa.com

Distributed in the US by Hachette Book Group
1290 Avenue of the Americas, 4th & 5th Floors,
New York, NY 10104

Distributed in Canada by Canadian Manda Group
664 Annette Street, Toronto, Ontario, Canada M6S 2C8

Publisher: Alison Starling
Editorial Director: Zena Alkayat
Commissioning Editors: Zara Anvari and Ellie Corbett
Managing Editor: Rachel Silverlight
Editor: Jenny Dye
Art Director: Ben Gardiner
Design: JC Lanaway
Production Manager: Caroline Alberti

Ilex is proud to partner with Tate; supporting the gallery
in its mission to promote public understanding and
enjoyment of British, modern and contemporary art.

ISBN 978-1-78157-668-7

A CIP catalogue record for this book
is available from the British Library

Printed and bound in China

10 9 8 7 6 5 4 3 2 1

Project photography by Colette Whittington

Additional credits:
Page 7 above image: Tate, London 2020 © Succession
Picasso/DACS, London 2020; 7 below image: Tate,
London 2020 © Robert Rauschenberg Foundation/VAGA
at ARS, NY and DACS, London 2020; 8 above and below
© Ellen Gallagher. Courtesy Gagosian.

Disclaimer

Project:
Print

30 projects to spark your creativity

Colette Whittington

ilex

Contents

Introduction   6

Relief Printing   **10**

Relief Printing Techniques   12

01. Metropolis Mail   14

02. Something from Nothing
Gift Bags   18

03. Folk Totes   20

04. Retro Arcade Pillow   24

05. Rolling Pin Wrapping Paper   28

06. Ocean Postcards   32

07. Glam Gift Tags   36

08. Tattoo You   40

09. Protest Print   44

10. Club Tropicana   48

11. Take a Picture   52

12. Curious Tea Towels   56

13. Mini Still Life   60

Screen Printing   **64**

Screen Printing Techniques   66

14. Colour Blur Placemats   70

15. Strike a Pose Scarf   74

16. Papercut Bunting   80

17. Out of this World Cushion   86

18. Into the Woods Wall Frieze   90

19. Fiesta Invitations   94

20. Doodlebug Napkins   98

21. Say Yes! T-shirt   102

22. Retro Tech Pencil Case   106

23. Dada Photomontage Book   112

24. Pop! Drawstring Bag   116

25. Punk Apron   120

Transfer Printing   **124**

Transfer Printing Techniques   126

26. Faded Memories   128

27. Freestyle Wall Tiles   130

28. Sunny Day Journal   132

29. Photographic Cyano Prints   136

30. Cosmic Lamp   140

Acknowledgements   144

01

02

03

04

05

06

07

08

09

10

11

12

13

14

15

16

17

18

19

20

21

22

23

24

25

26

27

28

29

30

Introduction

In its simplest form, printmaking is the transfer of ink from one surface to another, often from a block, printing plate or screen. The 'reveal' of the impression is one of the joys of this medium, and it has inspired artists for centuries. Printmaking is a vast topic covering a wide range of processes, some of which can be technically complex and require the support of a specialist workshop. The 30 projects in this book offer an easy, low-cost introduction to methods that can be readily practised at home.

Printmaking has survived throughout history partly due to its collaborative nature. A printmaker will not often work in isolation, and studios or workshops are spaces for artists to share knowledge and exchange ideas. This philosophy has enabled print to evolve in a world where technological advances can so easily overcome tradition. Today, printmaking spans both high art and popular culture. Print can be found on everything, from stencilled guerrilla graphics to museum-sponsored billboards and laser-printed cupcakes, badges, bags, floor tiles and wallpaper installations. The list is almost endless; prints are a significant and striking link between the museum and the marketplace, the establishment and the everyday.

Before the invention of photography, prints brought works of art to the masses, as artists would often employ engravers to reproduce their paintings. Many artists also made prints themselves, for example, Rembrandt Harmenszoon van Rijn, who mastered the process of etching. But it was Pablo Picasso who was the godfather of the new wave of mid-twentieth-century printmaking. Practising methods such as etching, lithography and linocut, crossing boundaries between disciplines and discovering ground-breaking techniques en route, he is often credited for inventing reduction lino printing. Later, the explosion of pop art in the 1950s and 1960s brought the commercial method of screen printing to the forefront as Andy Warhol, Eduardo Paolozzi and Robert Rauschenberg used the technique in diverse, bold and dynamic ways.

Portrait of a Woman after
Cranach the Younger
by Pablo Picasso, 1958
(Linocut on paper) Tate

Pledge
by Robert Rauschenberg, 1968
(Lithograph on paper) Tate

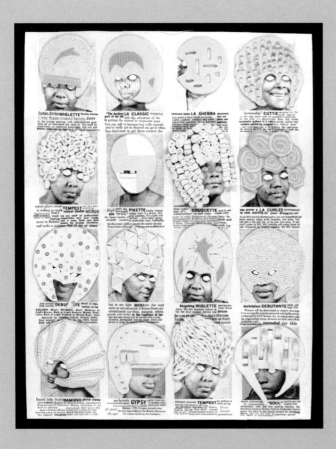

Above:
DeLuxe
by Ellen Gallagher, 2004-5
(Portfolio of 60
photogravure, etching,
aquatint and drypoint with
lithography, screenprint,
embossing, tattoo-machine
engraving, laser cutting
and chine collé; some with
additions of Plasticine,
paper collage, enamel,
varnish, gouache, pencil,
oil, polymer, watercolour,
pomade, velvet, glitter,
crystals, foil paper, gold
leaf, toy eyeballs and
imitation ice cubes) Tate

Left:
Detail from *DeLuxe*

Try your hand at Picasso's reduction lino printing technique (page 60), cutting the relief away from the lino as you overlay colours on top of one another. This technique not for the cautious and success will favour the bold. Discover how to make an exposure unit using photo-sensitive emulsion (pages 67–8) to reproduce commercial silk screen printing in your own home, making bold graphic statements like Warhol and Paolozzi did. Capture, too, the exuberant spirit of Frank Stella's multifaceted prints by drawing directly onto a silk screen with drawing fluid to make linear marks and build imagery (pages 94 and 98).

Taking inspiration from Ellen Gallagher, you can be playful and explore surface pattern and colour while highlighting serious issues and making your voice heard (page 44). Acetone transfer printing couldn't be simpler as demonstrated on pages 112 and 128. Rauschenberg used this method to transfer elements of newspapers and magazines to his 'Combine' prints, which became time capsules of the era in which they were created.

This book covers three main areas of printing: relief, screen and transfer. Each project identifies the materials and tools needed. Use the book as an introduction to different print methods, building up to more expensive specialist equipment after you have mastered the simpler techniques. All the projects have been adapted for home use through my experience of teaching print workshops over many years. To get you started, design ideas and templates have been provided. Naturally the more experienced artists among you may prefer to use your own designs, but for those of you who are beginners, as your skills improve your confidence will grow and independent ideas will begin to emerge. The common strand running through many of the projects is how to use 'low-fi' materials in imaginative ways, allowing you to customise items for your home and gifts for your family and friends.

Printmaking is one of the least intimidating art practices for a beginner to start and become accomplished in. It is also such good fun.

All you need to do is clear the kitchen table, roll up your sleeves and get stuck in!

Relief
Printing

Relief printmaking is one of the simplest and most democratic of all the print processes. It is a low-cost option that does not need much equipment, so it is easy to do at home on your kitchen table. In recent times, it has become a popular craft as it can be mastered relatively quickly given some guidance and handy tips.

A relief plate is generally one that has been carved, gouged or cut out to leave your design standing proud 'in relief' of the background. The negative spaces – the grooves or parts cleared – are taken away so they do not hold ink when the plate is inked up. The inked-up positive marks and shapes – the relief design – form the image that prints.

Relief plates, stamps and blocks can be made from a number of inexpensive materials, including erasers, polystyrene, corrugated cardboard and wood. Another suitable material is craft foam, which comes in thin sheets. Some of the projects also show you how to use lino plates, which are made of linoneum and can be carved using lino cutting tools. This chapter will encourage you to develop your crafting skills by becoming more familiar with the properties of the materials you are using.

We have been making relief prints most of our lives without even realising it, from early endeavours with potato prints in school to footsteps in the sand. Yet despite these humble origins, designs for relief printing can be as complex as you want them to be. The imagery you create can be as wild and fanciful as your imagination can conjure.

This chapter's projects will help you understand the processes involved in creating a relief stamp, block or plate. You will become equipped with the skills and confidence to experiment with your own design ideas and be able to overcome any technical difficulties you encounter along the way.

Relief Printing Techniques

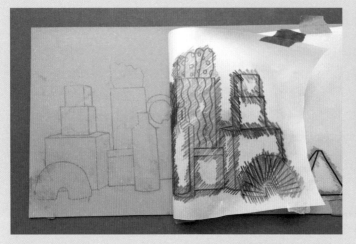

TRANSFERRING IMAGES ONTO LINO

If you are using lino to make your relief plate, you can transfer designs onto it with carbon paper. This is available from art and stationery stores, and it is coated with a thin layer of carbon or another pigmented substance. To use it, lay a sheet of carbon paper shiny side down on your lino. Place a piece of paper with your design on top, and go over the image with a ballpoint pen or sharp HB pencil to transfer an impression onto the lino. However, some vinyl lino plates do not receive the impression very well. A reliable alternative method is the 'scribble method'.

Build up 'scribbled' pencil marks close together on the reverse of the image with a soft pencil (2B or softer). Flip the image back over the correct way, secure it to the lino, and retrace the design with a ballpoint pen or sharp HB pencil. The pressure of the pen or pencil will release a transfer from the scribbled marks.

After using either carbon paper or the 'scribble method', you can then define the faint line with permanent marker before using lino cutting tools to remove the negative spaces on the lino.

If you're working with a photocopy, you can iron it onto the surface of the lino to transfer your image, as in the Take a Picture project on page 52.

INKING UP

A good print made from a relief plate, stamp or block relies on good inking up. I have used water-based inks and water-washable oil-based inks because they yield strong colour and are the ideal viscosity to roll onto the plate. They are also easy to wash up, without the need for harsh chemicals.

To ink up the design, roll out a small amount of ink on an ink tray with a brayer (a hand roller). Extend the ink in both directions to warm it up and to coat the whole of the brayer evenly. The ink should be quite stiff, otherwise it will fill up the grooves and cut marks made on your plate and fine details may be lost. Roll the brayer over your design plate back and forth several times until it has an even coverage of ink.

BURNISHING

Relief prints can be printed without a press by burnishing them. To do this, gently press down the paper onto the inked plate and rub firmly with a burnisher or baren – a smooth disc-shaped object. There are several types of baren on the market to suit all budgets. I often use a bamboo-leaf one as I like the feel of it in my hand, but a wooden spoon with a flat bottom will also work very well. Burnishing works best on lightweight paper, as it is difficult to apply enough pressure to transfer the ink successfully onto thicker paper.

DRYING TIME

Water-washable oil-based inks have many advantages, but one disadvantage is their drying time, which can be several days if you are printing multiple colours over each other. However, you can mix a couple of drops of a cobalt or manganese drier into the inks prior to inking up, which significantly speeds up the drying time. Refer to the manufacturer's instructions to mix the correct ratio. If you are printing multiple colours, let the first layer dry thoroughly before printing over it.

WASHING UP

When you have made your prints, wash your brayer and ink tray with liquid soap and water. I find it much easier to do this by adding the soap first and working it into the inky surfaces before adding the water. For water-washable oil-based inks, you can use cooking oil and a rag to clear unwanted ink away. Work the oil into the ink and wipe it away with a rag. You can then use soap and water to clear away any remaining residue.

HANDY TIP
Some good advice I heard in a print studio once was that the rolled ink should resemble the texture of velvet – tiny tacky peaks which have a distinctive soft cracking sound when rolled.

01. Metropolis Mail

If you are a complete beginner, this is the perfect starting point to help you discover the joy of printmaking. The materials and tools required are readily available and relatively cheap, and they will likely be familiar to you already. This is also a good project if space is limited. Erasers are so small all you need is a bit of elbow room for printing, and pigment ink pads keep the mess to a minimum. Take inspiration from architectural details found in the city to practise your carving skills and craft your own mini metropolis.

Materials and tools

Erasers of various sizes
Permanent marker pen
Small V-shaped lino cutter
Craft knife
Black pigment ink pad
Gradient pigment ink pad
Scrap paper
Damp cloth
Coloured card blanks
Coloured envelopes

1.

Collect a variety of erasers to use as blocks for your stamps. If you shop around you'll be surprised by how many different shapes and sizes you will be able to find. Draw your designs directly onto the erasers with a permanent marker pen.

2.

Use a small V-shaped lino cutter to gouge out your designs. This type of carving tool is perfect for the small scale of this task. The lines you score will be in recess and will not appear in the print. The areas you leave behind will be in relief and will appear in the print. Carefully hold the eraser on your print table with one hand, holding the cutter at a 45-degree angle to the drawn line. Cut grooves into the eraser following the lines you have made.

3.

To carve out any large shapes around the edges, use a craft knife to trace around the outline of your design. Carving from the sides of the eraser and pushing the blade in at about 3 mm (⅛ in) from the designed face of the block, slowly whittle small pieces of the background away. Take care to avoid your fingers. Continue to clear the background away until your design is defined in relief. Go back into your design with the V-shaped lino cutter to gouge out any further details.

4.

Test your eraser stamps by pushing them into an ink pad and stamping them ink side down onto scrap paper. Clear away any imperfections on your block. When you stamp on the paper, apply a small amount of pressure, but don't rock the stamp from side to side as parts of the background may print. Clean your stamps with a damp cloth to change colour or store them for later use.

5.

When you have practised your stamping technique, you are ready to print your metropolis stationery. I used two different ink pads for variety – a black one and a blue gradient one. To keep the colours defined when using a gradient ink pad, make sure that when you replenish your stamp with ink, the stamp hits the same spot on the gradient each time. This will prevent the colours mixing together. Experiment with different compositions and combinations of stamps on coloured card blanks and envelopes to customise your designs.

02. Something from Nothing Gift Bags

Mark-making in print is such a primal way to make an impression. This project taps into this direct way of working while challenging you to think about the print potential of every object in your home. Using low-fi, recyclable and humble materials can bring great satisfaction, relying on just your hands and imagination to turn the mundane into an innovative surface design. Get creative transforming plain paper bags into special gift versions in this eco-conscious project.

Materials and tools

Household objects and materials
  in a range of textures
  and shapes
Wooden blocks or foam card
Craft glue
Water-based relief printing
  ink in several colours
Ink trays
Brayers
Scrap paper
Cloth
Plain brown paper bags
  with handles

2.
Mount your different 'found' textures onto wooden blocks or foam card with craft glue. In the examples here I used corrugated cardboard, netting, string and dried spaghetti. Experiment and be imaginative. Some surfaces will work really well while others won't. This project is all about trial and error.

1.
Gather potential printmaking materials from around your home. Look for materials with interesting textures or objects with distinct shapes. Don't choose anything too precious as it may be damaged by the printing ink.

HANDY TIP
Try out your found objects and handmade blocks on scrap paper first; the results of this project are often quite surprising. The golden rules are don't over-ink and apply enough pressure – hold the stamp down and press hard for several seconds.

3.

Roll out your inks using a separate brayer for each colour. Less is more in this process; try not to over-ink your stamps, and remember that the more you use them, the more ink they will be holding. If you decide you want to use a stamp in another colour halfway through, blot it on scrap paper to remove excess ink. Use a damp cloth to clear the remaining ink from the surface.

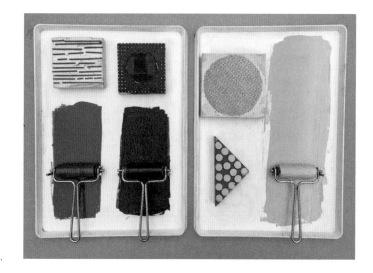

4.

To overprint, allow your bags to dry in between each layer. If you work on several bags at a time this shouldn't interrupt your creative flow too much. As the inks used here are water-based they should dry quite quickly, enabling you to keep the momentum going.

03. Folk Totes

I love printmaking with blocks as the possibilities are almost endless and the materials are inexpensive. The results can be surprisingly sophisticated, which is why adapting this time-honoured tradition using low-cost craft materials gives me so much pleasure. It is a fabulous way to hone your all-round printmaking skills. In this project you will learn how to cut craft foam to make print blocks, how to ink them up and how to explore your design ideas – fundamental skills for all printmakers. Taking its inspiration from folk designs, this funky tote project can be completed in just one day.

Materials and tools

Craft foam sheet
Ballpoint pen
Permanent marker pen
Cutting mat
Craft knife
All-purpose glue
Wooden blocks (to fit
  the designs)
Water-washable oil-based
  relief printing inks
  in 2 colours
2 ink trays
2 small brayers
Plain tote bag
Scrap paper

1.
Photocopy the templates provided on page 23 to get you started. You could also try drawing some of your own folk patterns to add to the mix and personalise your bag.

2.
Place your paper photocopy or drawing on top of the craft foam and trace over it firmly with a ballpoint pen. This will leave an impression on the foam that you can define with a permanent marker pen. Cut out the shapes on top of a cutting mat with a craft knife. A sharp blade will easily cut through the foam.

3.
Glue your foam shapes to the wooden blocks. These could be offcuts or even children's building blocks. The ones I used are around 1.5 cm (½ in) thick, but you could use thicker ones.

4.

Do a test run on paper so you can try out a few layouts. Roll your first printing ink on an ink tray, but don't roll out too much; look for a smooth, consistent texture that makes a crackling sound when rolled. Apply the ink evenly to your first block with the brayer. Repeat with the second colour, and build the design by stamping all of the blocks in turn on the paper. Once you have committed a block to a colour, keep it that colour if you want to finish the project in one day.

5.

Once you are ready to get started on the bag, place your first inked block face down onto the tote bag and apply pressure. Hold it down for several seconds before removing it to reveal your print. If you have two ink trays on the go you can be more fluid in deciding where your next block print will go.

6.

Alternate colours to suit your taste. It is best not to overlap a block print on top of another colour until the bottom colour is dry.

04. Retro Arcade Pillow

This project relies on the unifying effect of a tessellated repeat pattern for its impact. You will translate retro arcade-style graphics onto relief blocks designed to connect with each other. The overall pattern works seamlessly, using pixelated motifs in two scales, with different-coloured inks helping to highlight the repeat. This is a wonderfully simple project that looks much more complicated than it is. Easy to complete in a day, your pillow can be ready for bedtime.

Materials and tools

Pencil
Paper
Craft foam sheet
Craft knife
Cutting mat
1-cm (3/8-in) pre-cut craft foam mosaic squares
All-purpose glue (if your craft foam does not have a sticky back)
2 × 9-cm (3 1/2-in) square wooden blocks
Pillowcase and pillow
Thick paper or card
Water-based printing inks or acrylic paint in 2 colours
Textile printing medium
2 mixing containers and spoons
2 ink trays
2 brayers

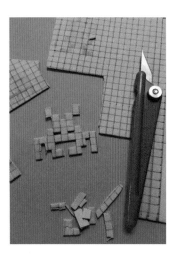

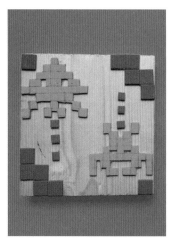

1.

Use the the templates on page 27 or plan your own on paper. If you're making your own design, make sure the edges of the motifs align with the edges of the wooden blocks. On a cutting mat, cut the smaller character motifs out of craft foam with a craft knife. You will arrange the larger motifs directly onto the wooden blocks from pre-cut craft foam squares.

2.

Transfer your craft foam pieces to the wooden blocks. Some craft foam comes with a sticky back so your designs can be stuck directly onto the wooden blocks. Alternatively, use a little all-purpose glue to adhere the foam to the block. Don't use too much as you don't want any glue seepage to interfere with the printing of your design.

3.

Insert cardboard or thick paper into the pillowcase to stop ink bleeding through to the reverse side. To prepare the ink, either mix regular water-based printing ink with a textile printing medium or mix acrylic paint with the medium. The mixture should have some viscosity. Add the medium in stages to prevent it from becoming too runny.

4.

Ink up your prepared wooden relief blocks. You will need two ink trays and two rollers for this so that your colours stay true and you can build your repeated print efficiently. Pass the ink over the surface of the foam to create an even coverage. As the craft foam stands proud of its wooden base, in relief, this is the area that will receive the ink.

5.

Make a repeat pattern by hand pressing the blocks face down onto the pillowcase. Use the edge of the pillowcase as a guide to help your design stay aligned. Use your full weight to press down onto each block and leave it on the surface of the fabric for several seconds before releasing to allow time for the ink to penetrate the fibres.

6.

As you work along the pillowcase, butt the subsequent block up against the previous one before you release the first one. This will help your design stay aligned when you leave the edge of the pillowcase. Follow the instructions on the textile medium for how to iron your pillowcase to 'cure' or heat-set the ink. This will ensure that your printed design is stable and can be laundered.

05. Rolling Pin Wrapping Paper

Roller printing is such good fun – seeing your design translated into an almost effortless repeated pattern is incredibly satisfying. The process was initially used for the production of wallpapers. The roller action creates a repeat print that keeps on going until the ink runs out. Once you have mastered the technique of applying the right amount of ink to the roller, this method can be applied to fabric for fashion garments, tote bags, home furnishings and much more. In this project you will create a hand-rolled wrapping paper with a repeat pattern to personalise special gifts.

Materials and tools

Paper
Pencil
Ruler
2 rolling pins of
  different lengths
Scissors
Craft foam sheet
Double-sided sticky tape
Craft knife
Cutting mat
Brown parcel paper
Masking tape
Water-based relief printing ink
Brayer
Ink tray
Scrap paper

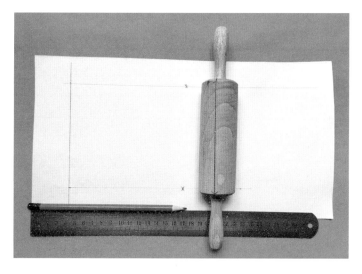

1.

Create a paper guide to ensure your design fits the first rolling pin. Draw a straight line down the length of the rolling pin with a pencil and ruler. Measure the length and, on the paper, draw parallel lines the same distance apart as the length of the rolling pin, with a perpendicular line at one end to create a three-sided rectangle. Next, mark a full rotation of the rolling pin. Line up the pencil on the rolling pin with the starting edge of your rectangle. Roll the pin along the parallel lines and mark the end of one full rotation on each line. Join the marks to form a box shape and cut it out.

2.

Draw around the paper guide onto the craft foam. Cut the box shape out of the foam. Cover the back of the foam with double-sided sticky tape, but don't take the tape protector off yet. Trim off any excess that overhangs the sides.

3.

Draw your design ideas directly onto the front of the foam (the side without the tape). Cut them out with scissors or a craft knife on a cutting mat, depending on how complex your designs are.

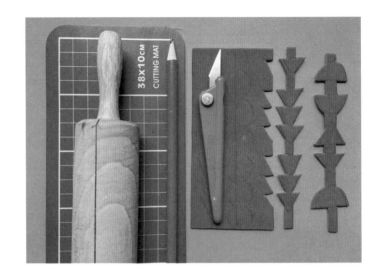

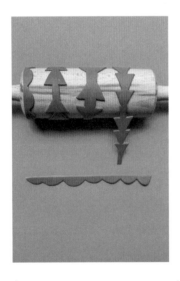

4.

Attach your foam shapes to the rolling pin by removing the tape backing and pressing firmly against the rolling pin. Use your pencil guideline as a starting point and roll your design around the pin.

5.

After you have wrapped your shape around the circumference of the rolling pin, trim off any excess foam to make the shape sit flush on the roller.

6.

Tape the corners of the brown paper to your work surface. Use a brayer to roll out a small amount of ink onto your tray. Pass the brayer through the ink several times until the ink has spread out and the tray has an even coverage. Pass the rolling pin through the ink back and forth on the tray several times until it has an even coverage of ink.

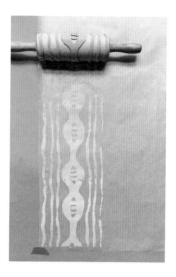

7.

Roll the pin over the paper away from you. Have plenty of scrap paper on hand to practise on before you commit to your good paper. As you roll away from yourself the ink will become lighter as it begins to run out. You could replenish the ink when it starts to run out, although you may find it hard to line the pattern up again, so it might be best to accept some imperfections!

8.

Take your second rolling pin and repeat steps 1–7 for a second design. You can add different designs to different-sized rolling pins, and have fun creating easy repetitions.

9.

Lots of different materials and textures will hold ink and make a print impression. This low-cost upcycling technique will get you thinking about how you can use ordinary household materials to make prints. Experiment by adding different shapes to your rolling pins.

POST CARD

TO: _____

_____

POSTCODE: _____

POST CARD

TO: _____

_____

POSTCODE: _____

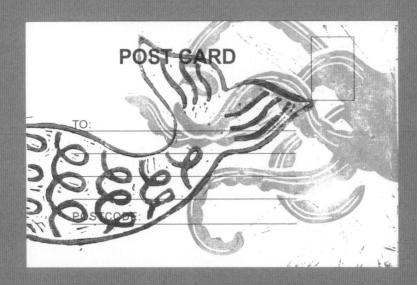

POST CARD

TO: _____

_____

POSTCODE: _____

06. Ocean Postcards

This is a really simple project to help you get to grips with the idea of making designs using positive and negative line and space. In lino printing, the line you cut away does not print – only the plate left behind holds the ink. All great printmakers in lino have mastered this principle, with their designs often built around the use of positive and negative space. With a bit of practice and confidence you can begin to think like a master printmaker too.

Materials and tools

Pencil or crayon
Paper
Permanent marker
Soft pencil
Ballpoint pen or sharp HB pencil
3 soft-cut lino plates, A4
  (US letter) size
Lino cutters, various sizes
Craft knife
Cutting mat
Water-based relief printing ink
Ink trays
Brayer
Blank postcards
Burnisher, wooden block
  or large spoon

1.

Draw sea-themed designs for your postcards, paying attention to positive and negative space, or use the templates on page 35. The mermaid tail (a) is the drawing for the design. If we cut out the black line to cut, our print would look like b – the line would be negative. If we want the drawn line to print, to be the positive line, we will have to cut all of the red area away as shown in c.

2.

Go over your design in permanent marker. Before you begin to cut your designs out of the lino, use a pencil or crayon to colour in different positive and negative combinations to discover the approach you like best.

3.

To transfer the design onto lino, scribble with a soft pencil onto the back of your drawing and lay it scribble-side down on top of the lino. With a ballpoint pen or HB pencil, trace over your drawing; the pressure will transfer the pencil onto the lino, leaving a faint tracing of your design. To make the drawing easier to see on the lino, go over it with a permanent marker.

HANDY TIP
Don't cut your lino pieces too small. The burnishing technique (see page 13) does not work well on tiny pieces of lino as they move around too much under the pressure being applied and this can spoil the clarity of your print.

4.

Transfer the mermaid-tail design onto the lino twice. Cut out the positive line by clearing all the spaces between the black lines on the first tail. Then cut out the black marker line on the second tail so that the negative and positive spaces are reversed. Cut around each design with a craft knife on a cutting mat, leaving a border of approximately 5 mm (¼ in), but don't disturb the outer edge of the image. Repeat this process for the octopus and sun designs.

5.

Ink up your lino blocks by passing an even coat of printing ink over the surface of the lino with a brayer. Too much ink will fill in your carefully carved-out lines and might make the paper slip when you print, so be careful with the application.

6.

Finally, burnish your postcards by placing them face down onto the inked-up plate, and rub in a circular motion with a burnisher, wooden block or the back of a spoon. You will get a better result if you stand up and apply good pressure to the block.

TEMPLATES
Photocopy onto A4 (US letter) paper at 100%

07. Glam Gift Tags

Making your own tags is a fantastic way to make the gifts you give feel more personal. You could theme your design to complement the gift or simply create a stash of tags that you can use any time. This project offers a way of elevating your ideas even further by using embossing powders to add a touch of pizzazz to your gifts. Enjoy building glittery embossed textures with this easy-to-master technique. This is such a satisfying and quick way of stamping with inks, and you can have lots of fun experimenting with different designs.

Materials and tools

Erasers in sizes to suit your gift tags
Plain gift tags
Pencil
Lino cutters, fine and medium
Craft knife
Cutting mat
Scrap paper
Coloured pigment ink pad
Embossing ink pad
Embossing powder
Embossing heat gun

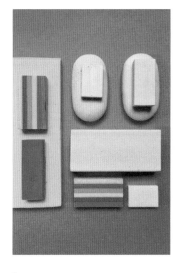

1.
Gather different-sized erasers. If you can only find small ones, adjust your designs to fit the scale of the erasers. If your erasers are large, cut them to size with a craft knife on a cutting mat. If you can only find erasers with rounded faces, stay away from the edges as cutting your design out of this area may spoil your print.

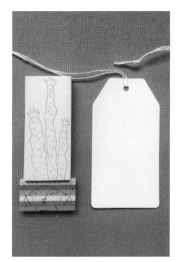

2.
Plan your design on paper with the size of the gift tags you are using in mind. For this project we are using one ink pigment and one embossing powder – so we need two different components to the design. Draw your designs onto the erasers.

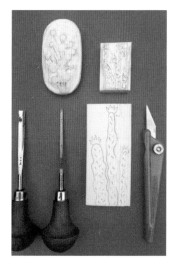

3.
Cut out the background from your designs using a fine lino cutter and a craft knife. This is a relief print, so the area you want to print needs to sit proud of its background. Clear away any unwanted background areas carefully, using a slightly larger lino cutter for this if necessary.

4.

Due to the small scale of these gift tag stamps, it is a good idea to test them out first so that you can clear away any unwanted elements. Use your black or coloured pigment ink pad to do this rather than using the embossing powder. Press your stamps into the ink pad and then stamp them onto a piece of scrap paper.

5.

Print the first part of your design onto the gift tags with an ink pad. I have carved vase designs to stamp in green. When dry, stamp your second stamp, the foliage in the vase in my case, into the clear embossing ink pad. Press hard and allow the fluid to impregnate the eraser. Stamp in place onto your gift tag.

6.

The mark left by the embossing fluid will be very faint but just clear enough for you to see it. Sprinkle the embossing powder over your design and then shake off the excess, which can be carefully swept back into the powder pot.

7.

Hold an embossing heat gun at a 45-degree angle to the tag. The tags are flammable and the gun gets hot, so be careful. As the powder heats, it melts and forms an embossed (raised) area where you have stamped. Be careful not to overheat the powdered print impression as you can easily 'melt off' the embossing powder.

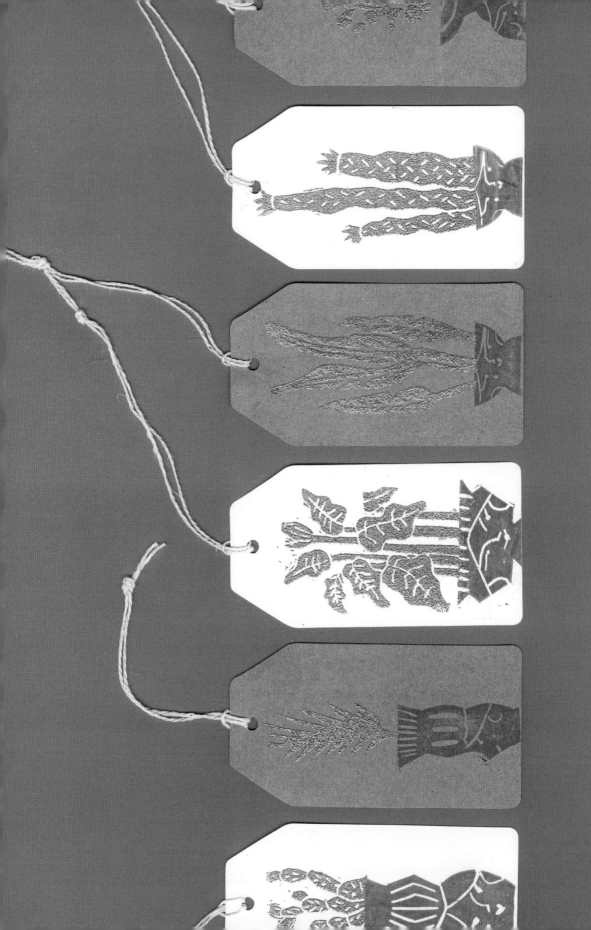

08. Tattoo You

This project is an interactive and fun way to explore lino cutting and block printing. Taking inspiration from vintage sailor tattoos, the tattoo templates provided will help you hone your lino-cutting skills. It is the perfect project to help you understand how the cut lino line works, while changing your look and impressing friends with your new body art. And if you prefer to create your own temporary tattoo designs, let your creativity flow!

Materials and tools

Pencil
Paper
Permanent marker pen
Soft pencil or carbon
  transfer paper
Soft-cut lino plates
Lino cutters, various sizes
Craft knife
Cutting mat
Wooden stamping blocks
  to fit designs
Sandpaper
All-purpose glue
Handles or knobs for blocks
  (optional)
Water-based, child-friendly
  relief printing ink
Brayer
Ink tray
Damp cloth

1.

Before you start, apply a tiny amount of the ink to a patch of your skin, avoiding your eyes and face, and leave for a day to check that it does not cause a reaction. Plan your designs in pencil or use the templates on page 43. The black lines will be cut out of the lino and your design will print in reverse. Use a marker pen to make the lines thicker.

2.

Transfer your designs onto the lino plates by using carbon transfer paper or the scribble transfer method (see page 12). A faint line will transfer onto the lino. Go over this line with a permanent marker to make it easier to see and cut with your lino tools.

3.

Use a fine lino cutting tool to cut out the black line. Try to apply even pressure to the cut throughout, turning the lino around to carve out intricate detail or organic lines. With a clearing cutter or a U-shaped tool, clear a couple of centimetres (half an inch) around the design and then cut the excess away with a craft knife on a cutting mat.

Be careful during this stage not to be overzealous with your clearing – you don't want to nick the outer shape of your design.

4.

Lightly sand the surface and edges of the wooden blocks to remove any splinters. Use an all-purpose glue to adhere each lino design to the surface of a wooden block. Mop up any glue left on the wood. Allow to dry fully. You may decide to attach a handle to the reverse of your block using all-purpose glue.

5.

Ink up your stamping blocks with water-based, child-friendly inks. Using a small brayer, roll an even coat of ink over the surface of the stamps. Use a damp cloth to clean up any ink that falls on the wooden surface.

6.

Practise inking up and stamping your blocks on paper first to identify any imperfections. It is common to leave unwanted fragments of lino behind when clearing, as seen in the practice prints above. Use a lino cutter to remove the small marks around the designs.

7.

Finally, stamp firmly onto dry skin, avoiding your face and eyes. Rock the stamp slowly around the body's contours. Have a damp cloth on hand in case you need to start over a couple of times. The ink will take 15–20 minutes to dry, or you can speed this up with a hairdryer. The tattoos will wash off with water.

09. Protest Print

There is something so visually direct about a single-colour lino print that it lends itself to clear, no-nonsense messages such as those used on protest placards. Easy-carve blocks are also a great way to make graphic, bold designs that mimic woodcut prints, as the thick carving block allows you to dig a little deeper, adding expression into your cut marks. Stay true to this raw way of working and create your own protest poster. Combine text and imagery to make your voice heard. Resist clearing the block too much to leave the mark of the maker and create a bold statement.

Materials and tools

Easy-carve block, smaller than
  A4 (US letter) size
Paper, A4 (US letter) size
Pencil
Permanent marker
Light box (optional)
Masking tape (if not using
  light box)
Carbon paper, A4 (US letter) size
Lino cutters, various sizes
Large brayer
Water-washable oil-based
  relief printing ink
Ink tray
Thick cartridge paper,
  A4 (US letter) size
Burnisher
Letter stamps
Pigment ink pad

1.

If you are using the template on page 47, skip steps 1 and 2. Draw round your easy-carve block onto paper to mark the dimensions of your design. Sketch your protest design in the box, combining text and imagery. Trace over the pencil line with a permanent marker once you are happy with your final design.

2.

To prepare your image, flip it over on a light box and trace it again on the reverse of the paper. Alternatively, tape your image to a back-lit window if you don't have access to a light box.

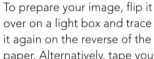

3.

Place the carbon paper on the easy-carve block. Place your image on top so that any text appears backwards. Go over all lines with a pen or pencil, pressing firmly and keeping everything in position. Define the resulting carbon lines on your block with the marker.

4.

The beauty of the easy-carve block is that you can make deep grooves and carve in a very free way without cutting through the plate. In this example I have tried to leave traces of the cuts behind and not clean up the outline of the image too much, as I enjoy the naive aesthetic.

5.

Using a large brayer big enough to cover the plate, ink up your design with the relief printing ink. Ensure you use good inking-up technique (see page 12). It may take a couple of attempts to get the technique right; a common mistake is to over-ink the block.

6.

Lay your cartridge paper on top of the inked-up block, taking care to align it so that the plate is central. Transfer your design to the paper by burnishing on the back. Rub in circular movements with the burnisher, applying firm pressure to all areas.

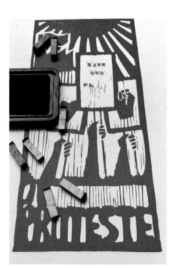

7.

Peel the paper off carefully and allow to dry. Oil-based inks take longer to dry than water-based inks, so don't be alarmed if the print takes several days to dry properly. Water-based inks can be used with this plate, but I wanted the ink to be bolder and carry a slight gloss on the paper. Experiment to discover your preference.

8.

When your print is dry, try using letter stamps to personalise your poster or add further information. Letter stamps come in a wide range of fonts and will make a dynamic contrast to any hand-cut typography. I prefer to use pigment ink pads for small stamps, as the clarity is much better and the ink dries quickly. Using the same colour for your stamps as your print will help to unite the overall design.

Piña Colada

50ml coconut milk
50ml golden rum
75 ml fresh
    pineapple juice
2 tbsp sugar
    syrup
juice of 1/2
    lime
slice of
    pineapple
maraschino
cherry
ice

10. Club Tropicana

These deceptively easy-to-make cocktail party recipe cards will satisfy the colourist within you. By experimenting with your inking-up technique you can discover how to make impressive colour blends to transform your relief prints. No two colour blends will be exactly the same; give yourself over to the spontaneity of the process and this game of chance can be very rewarding. To get the party started, set up a 'make-your-own' drinks station. Provide your finished cards, with a cocktail or mocktail recipe written on each one, so your guests can use them to make their drinks.

Materials and tools

Plain paper, A4 (US letter) size
Permanent marker
Soft pencil
Ballpoint pen or sharp HB pencil
Soft-cut lino plate, A4
  (US letter) size
Lino cutters, various sizes
Craft knife
Cutting mat
Large brayer
Water-based relief printing ink
  in 3 bright colours
Large ink tray
Paper or cards to print
Burnisher

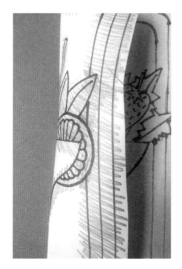

1.

Plan your design on paper to fit within the soft-cut A4 (US letter size) lino. Don't make the design too small as it will be difficult to read the recipe details. The template on page 51 features the cocktail glass cut out as a negative shape in which to write the cocktail recipe later. Define your drawing in marker pen and scribble on the back with a soft pencil (see page 12).

2.

Lay the drawing scribble-side down on top of the lino. With a ballpoint pen or sharp HB pencil, trace over your drawing; the pressure will transfer the pencil graphite onto the lino, leaving a faint tracing of your design on the surface. Go over the design in permanent marker to help you see the drawing more clearly.

3.

Use a fine or medium lino cutting tool to cut along the marker line. You can go back over your cut line later with a bigger blade to make the line bolder. I have done this to highlight the fruit and garnish. When clearing the glass shape, be careful not to dig too deep and create a hole. Use a craft knife to cut your lino to size on a cutting mat, leaving a 5-mm (¼-in) border.

4.

Now comes the fun part. Choose the colours you want to use in your blended colour gradient. Using the largest brayer you have, dab pea-sized blobs of coloured printing ink onto the rubber and position them so they touch each other.

5.

Roll the colours onto a large ink tray or piece of plastic. Keep the roller in the same position until you have extended the ink a little. Then, on both the forward and backwards action, move the brayer left and right a little to blend the colours further.

6.

Apply your inked-up roller to the lino plate by using the brayer in a forward action only. Every time you go back to the blended ink to charge your roller, ensure you match the position of the roller to the colour stripes you have created. This will stop the colours from blending too much and losing definition.

7.

Lay your paper on top of the inked-up plate and rub the back in circular movements with a burnisher. Water-based inks will dry quickly so you will need to work quite fast. Allow your design to dry. Fill in the card with the ingredients for your favourite cocktail or mocktail.

11. Take a Picture

Translating one of your photographs into an art print is very fulfilling: the cut marks add life to an otherwise static image. Expressive mark-making can create an atmosphere that enriches the subject of the photograph as the hand of the maker is present in the marks made. You will learn how to transfer a tonal image onto lino and depict it through the cut lines. This satisfying technique will transform your relief printing, liberating your mark-making to help you release your inner artist and find your own cutting style.

Materials and tools

Photocopy of a favourite
   holiday photograph
Soft-cut lino plate
Masking tape
Greaseproof paper
Scissors
Iron
Scrap piece of soft-cut lino
Lino cutters, various sizes
Scrap paper
Brayer
Ink tray
Water-washable oil-based
   relief printing ink
Burnisher
Medium-weight smooth
   cartridge paper

Take a Picture   2019 A·P C·W

1.

Choose a photograph that you would like to translate into a lino print. Pick an image that either has lots of texture in it or has strong lighting and pronounced shadows. Scale the image up or down to fit your piece of lino using a photocopier. I used an A4 (US letter) sized piece of soft-cut lino.

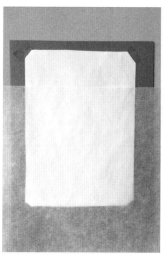

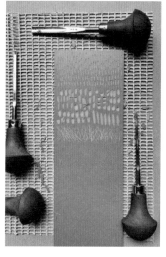

2.

Tape your photocopy face down on the lino and place greaseproof paper over the top. Set your iron to a medium heat and iron over the paper, applying moderate pressure. Be careful at this stage; if you think the lino is distorting or sticking, remove the iron immediately. The aim is to encourage the photocopy toner to transfer onto the lino.

3.

Keep working the back of the photocopy with the iron, occasionally carefully peeling up the corners to check your progress. When you feel you have a clear enough image to work from, remove the photocopy carefully. A transferred toner impression should be left on the surface of your lino.

4.

Before you begin to cut your image, practise your mark-making on a scrap piece of lino to explore the range and capabilities of the cutting tools you are using. Try to make each mark in one movement or with one flick of your tool. Ink up your tester piece with printing ink to examine the marks you have made.

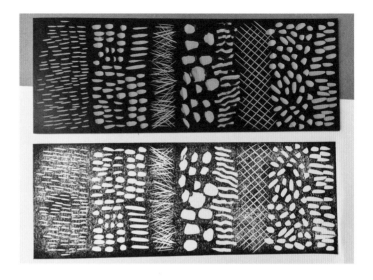

5.

Place a piece of scrap paper onto the lino, and burnish the back to create a test print of your marks. When you are satisfied you have a range of marks to capture your chosen image, you can begin to cut out your main lino plate.

6.

This project is all about making expressive marks, so try not to 'trace' the outline of the shapes in your photo. Instead, gouge out strong highlights with a series of expressive marks. Change the cutters you use for different parts of the image to make the overall effect more dynamic. The same principle applies if your photograph has lots of texture.

7.

Clean your print area thoroughly, making sure all the excess bits of lino are brushed away. Roll out a tray of printing ink and coat your brayer. Ink up your plate.

8.

To register and ensure your print is centred, tape a piece of scrap paper to your table. Make sure it is the same size as the paper you want to print onto. Hold the underneath or sides of the lino carefully, being careful not to disturb the inked-up surface. Place the inked-up plate in the middle of the paper, ink side up.

9.

You can nudge the plate left, right, up or down to make adjustments to its position. Line up your print paper with the edges of the base sheet and burnish the back of the paper over the area to be printed.

10.

Peel away the paper carefully to reveal your progress. If the image is uneven, put the paper back in position and carry on burnishing, applying more pressure to the patchy parts.

11.

When you are confident all the ink has been released from your lino plate, peel back your paper fully to reveal your expressive art print.

HANDY TIP
Oil-based inks take a few days to dry, so put your print somewhere safe until then to prevent it from smudging.

12. Curious Tea Towels

Many artists and creatives are avid collectors of 'curios'. From tin toys to ceramic ornaments and plastic dinosaurs, these objects hold memories and often provide inspiration. Pop artist Peter Blake has a fascinating private collection of memorabilia, popular collectibles, taxidermy and one-of-a-kind curiosities, offering insight into his artistic obsessions. This project will guide you through the design process and registration for a two-coloured relief print on fabric, to create a bespoke tea towel that reflects your own curious collection of objects.

Materials and tools

Collection of small objects
Camera
Soft pencil or carbon paper
2 soft-cut lino plates, A3
  (US tabloid) size
Craft knife
Cutting mat
Ballpoint pen or sharp HB pencil
Permanent marker
U-shaped clearing tool, large
Lino cutters, various sizes
Plain tea towel, ironed
Strong tape or bulldog clips
Brayer
Water-washable oil-based relief
  printing inks in 2 colours
Ink tray
Burnisher

1.
Gather some small objects that mean something to you. They may bring back a memory or you might just like their material or shape. Lay them out in an arrangement. Place the objects quite close together – you don't want too much space in between them as this will affect your cutting of the plate later.

2.
Take a photograph from directly above the laid-out objects. Print out your photograph twice in black and white to A3 (US tabloid) size. In the next steps, you will use these print-outs as guides to help you create bold, simplified versions of the objects to print onto your tea towel.

3.
Lay a piece of carbon paper shiny side down on top of each lino plate, with a print-out on top. Alternatively, scribble on the reverse of the print-outs, and place each one right side up on a lino plate (see page 12).

4.

Line the photocopies up to fit exactly corner to corner on the plates. They must be the same size as your plates, so use a craft knife to cut your lino down to size if necessary on a cutting mat. Take one of the plates (we'll call this 'plate 1' from now on), and use a ballpoint pen or sharp HB pencil to draw a silhouetted line, slightly bigger than the actual outline, around each of your objects. On the second plate (we'll call this 'plate 2' from now on), trace the intricate details of each object. Tracing rather ironing the photocopies onto your lino will give you clear, defined lines to follow when you cut your lino in the next step. Go over the transferred carbon or graphite lines on both plates with a permanent marker.

5.

Use your lino cutting tools to carve both plates. Plate 1 will be the background, printed here in green, and will print block shapes of colour. Plate 2 will transfer the detail over the top, printed here in black.
Plate 1: Clear the space around your objects using a large U-shaped clearing tool. Don't worry too much about defining the line around your silhouettes; the background shapes do not need to match the originals exactly.
Plate 2: Again, clear the space around your objects with a large U-shaped clearing tool. Pay special attention to defining the outlines of your objects and picking out detail using your finer tools. Remember that the part you cut away will not print.

6.

When you have cut both plates, add some highlight marks to plate 1. These marks can be made approximately with a large tool. Don't get carried away here – these marks are meant to be highlight flourishes, and you don't want to cut too much of your green block shapes away. These cut lines will be white when printed.

7.

Place your tea towel face down on the work surface. Tape it along its long left-hand edge with strong tape or hold it in place with bulldog clips. Place the uninked plate 1 underneath the tea towel in the centre. Make tape or pencil marks on your work surface at two corners of the plate so that you will be able to register plate 2 in exactly the same position.

8.

Ink up plate 1 using printing ink. Register it using the tape guide marks. Lay the secured tea towel over the inked-up plate and burnish on the back. Peel the tea towel back carefully, keeping the taped edge in place. Allow to dry. As the ink is oil-based, this may take several days.

9.

Ink up plate 2 in black printing ink. Use the tape guide marks to place the plate on your work surface, and lay the secured tea towel over the top. Burnish on the reverse of the tea towel. Allow the print to dry.

13. Mini Still Life

The reduction linocut process used in this project was a method famously championed by Pablo Picasso in the 1950s. Sometimes called 'elimination printing', it involves cutting away a single lino block in stages and overprinting coloured layers. While Picasso's expressive cut marks make his prints look effortless, good planning in the design stage of this project is critical – once a section is cut away there is no going back! This technique is especially good with large lino plates. Using just one block to print multiple colours is cost-effective and makes the registration of the layers much easier. This technique can't be rushed because of the drying time in between the overprints, which gives you plenty of time to plot your next cut.

Materials and tools

Objects for still life arrangement
2 sheets of A3 (US letter) drawing paper
Pencil
Colouring pencils
Tracing paper, A3 (US letter) size
Permanent marker
Soft pencil
Soft-cut lino plate, A3 (US letter) size
Ballpoint pen or HB pencil
Eraser
Methylated spirit or acetone (optional)
V-shaped lino cutting tool
U-shaped clearing tool
Scrap paper
Masking tape
Water-washable oil-based relief printing inks in 3 colours
Ink tray
Large brayer
Small brayer
Burnisher
6-8 lightweight smooth archival printing paper sheets, larger than A3 (US letter) size

1.

Make a still life arrangement. Choose objects for their shape, form or texture.

2.

Make a drawing of your arrangement to the scale of the lino you are using. I used A3 (US letter) size. Do this freehand or print out a photograph of your still life to the right size and trace it on tracing paper. Colour it in using three colours and white. My drawing has been done with the help of a computer. When you are planning your colours, note that in reduction printing we generally start with the lightest colour. Don't make your colours too complex to begin with; aim for blocks of colour until you are confident with the process. The final colour applied is good for picking out details. If you have created your drawing on the computer, try out different colours until you are happy with your plan.

3.

Make a linear drawing of your colour plan on tracing paper with permanent marker. Scribble on the back with a soft pencil, flip the image over onto your lino and retrace with a ballpoint pen or HB pencil (see page 12). Your print will be the reverse image of your original, unless you flip your tracing paper line drawing before you transfer it.

4.

Go over the graphite lines on your lino with permanent marker and rub out the graphite with an eraser. At this point I also like to rub the marker lines with a little methylated spirit or acetone to remove excess ink as it sometimes transfers when you first print. If you are using methylated spirit or acetone, do so in a well-ventilated area away from open flames, and wear goggles and disposable gloves. Begin to cut your lino, starting with any areas you want to keep white. Use a V-shaped cutting tool to outline the shape you want to cut, and then use your U-shaped clearing tool to scoop out larger unwanted areas. Remember, only the relief areas left behind will hold the ink and print.

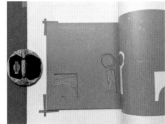

5.

Lay a piece of paper the same size as the printing paper onto your work surface. Mark its corners with tape. Centre the lino on the paper and mark its corners with tape. Ink up your first colour, register your lino on the base paper and line up your printing paper on top using the tape guides. Burnish firmly on the back.

6.

Make 6–8 prints of your first layer to perfect your burnishing technique and in case you make mistakes on later layers – remember, this stage cannot be repeated. Allow these prints to dry fully before you print on top of them. With oil-based inks this may take a couple of days. Refer to the manufacturer's instructions.

7.

Clean off the printing ink and begin to cut your next colour layer. In my example I want to print brown over the pink. To do this I must cut away all of the areas I want to remain pink. Any areas that I want to remain brown or blue I need to leave. Refer to your colour plan drawing for reference.

8.

Ink up your second colour on the lino, position it correctly using the registration marks, and register one of your prepared first prints on top. Burnish firmly on the back.

9.

Assess your print and troubleshoot any problems. You can clean your lino and cut away any unwanted lino grooves. Reprint this brown layer again over all of the pink prints you have prepared. Register each one in the same way, and continue to troubleshoot any glitches after each printing. Let each layer dry before printing the next.

10.

When you have printed your second colour, clean the lino and cut away the areas you want to remain brown. This will leave the highlight layer to be picked out in the final colour (blue, in my example). When your two-colour prints are dry, ink up the final colour. You may not have many relief areas left, so swap to a small brayer for inking up.

11.

Register the prints against your tape marks and burnish. This may take several attempts to perfect. You should have enough prints to get at least one perfect! This final layer will pull your design together and you should now have a cohesive three-colour reduction print.

Screen
Printing

Screen printing is a popular printmaking method that is commonplace in the fashion we wear, the homes we live in and the urban environments we frequent. In recent years it has had a huge renaissance as artists, designers and consumers have rediscovered its appeal in an age where handcrafted products are flourishing in reaction to mass production.

This method involves using a fabric mesh and stencil to block ink from parts of a printed surface. A squeegee is passed across the mesh of the screen, pushing ink through it onto a substrate (the material onto which you are printing). One colour is printed at a time but the substrate may be overprinted many times.

Screen printing is a satisfying and flexible technique; prints can be made simply with cut-out paper stencils or by using drawing fluids and fillers to transfer drawings onto the mesh of the screen. Photographic imagery can be reproduced to create photomontage impressions with text on top, or complex layering of colour and texture can be achieved.

This chapter will offer you a taster of the many ways to manipulate this versatile method, starting simply with easy-to-master 'low-fi' techniques, and moving on to the more sophisticated method of reproducing photographic imagery with a DIY exposure unit. All of the projects included are designed to work successfully in a home environment.

If you are a novice printmaker, working through the projects will help you build confidence. Screen printing, although sometimes simple, is not a method to be rushed, as washing out screens, waiting for impressions to dry and building up layers requires patience. This gives you lots of time to contemplate your next move, however, and consider future possibilities with the exciting new knowledge you have gained.

Screen Printing Techniques

FLOODING A SCREEN
Follow the instructions in each project to transfer your stencil to the screen. Before printing it is good practice to 'flood' your screen to fill the mesh with ink without making an impression. Pour a line of ink across the top of your screen on the frame side (the side with the recess). Lift your frame clear of the surface. Use the squeegee to pull the ink towards you in a 'flood' stroke. If you have a paper stencil this helps it to stick to the screen. 'Back flooding' is the same stroke with the ink pushed away from you. If you are making multiple prints and need to replenish the paper, back flooding will help prevent water-based ink drying in your screen in between prints. It is not always necessary to flood your screen and you may not want to if you are registering a tricky print and need to see through the mesh for the first pull.

GOOD PULLING TECHNIQUE
To make a good print it is essential to apply even pressure along the squeegee. Place your screen on the surface you are printing and pour a line of printing ink across the top of the screen. Angling the squeegee at 45 degrees to the mesh, pull the line of ink towards you. As you pull down, try to push the ink through the mesh evenly. To make another pass of the ink, push it away from you again with the squeegee at 45 degrees to the mesh and the ink line on the other side of the squeegee.

COATING A SCREEN WITH PHOTOGRAPHIC EMULSION
Some projects in this chapter use photographic emulsion and a DIY exposure unit to transfer the stencil image to the screen. If possible, coat your screen with the emulsion in a darkened room. Follow the manufacturer's instructions on how to mix up your emulsion. Many come with a sensitiser powder that needs to be added to the main mixture to activate it in advance.

As the emulsion is light-sensitive it is essential to work quickly to coat the screen and place it in a dark space to dry. When you are ready to get going, pour a line of emulsion across the width of the top of the screen, with the mesh side (the side without the recess) up. Pull the mixture down the length of the screen, holding the squeegee at a 45-degree angle and applying even

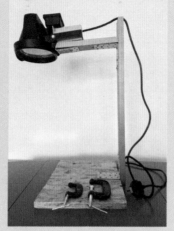

pressure along it. Repeat across the screen until it is covered. Holding your screen up, run the squeegee from top to bottom on the reverse of the mesh to scoop up any excess mixture. Return it to the emulsion pot. Repeat this on both sides of the mesh a couple of times to ensure a thin, even coat has been applied. Wipe away any residue in the frame with a cloth.

Place the coated screen in a dark place to dry, preferably flat. Ensure the photo emulsion pot has its lid secured and it is also stored in a dark place.

Light causes the photographic emulsion to harden and bind to the mesh. The areas covered by your design when you expose the screen are where your ink will pass through and make an impression when you print.

MAKING AN EXPOSURE UNIT

There are many ways to make your own exposure unit, with lots of online tutorials to help you create one that suits your needs and budget. Most require either a halogen or UV light to expose your screen and activate the emulsion. The exposure unit above required only some basic joinery skills, angle brackets, D clamps and a halogen lamp. I used scraps of wood to make a frame that would support my lamp in position 50 cm (20 in) away from the table and 45 cm (18 in) away from the screen as the frame depth is 5 cm (2 in). This is where you will have to get creative as your home set up may be different. The light could be hung from above for instance, or secured to a shelf. The important thing is to place the lamp 45 cm (18 in) above the top of the screen.

EXPOSING A SCREEN

Exposing a screen can be temperamental in a home environment. I strongly recommend you experiment with exposure times with your set-up in advance of your project. Different lamp types will alter the exposure time – UV light will be different from halogen, for example. You can use online exposure calculators as a guide if you need some reassurance to begin with. With the set-up I am using my standard exposure time is 8–20 minutes. This has worked really well for the strong, bold lines and shapes featured in this book.

In a darkened room, place your dry photo-emulsion-coated screen mesh side up on the exposure table. Lay your drawn, photocopied or cut-out images on top of the coated mesh. If there is text in the image place it on the screen back to front.

The images laid on top of the screen should be on acetate or made transparent with the baby oil method (see page 69). Secure the image in place with a large piece of glass or thick clear acrylic to weigh down the images, giving them good contact with the screen. This will ensure that no light creeps around the sides of the image, making it blurry.

Turn the light on and centre your screen so that the whole of the image is in the full field of light. Leave the room to protect your eyes and put a timer on for 8 minutes (or the exposure time that works for you). Turn the light off when the time is up and remove the glass and imagery. Wash out the screen as soon as possible to remove the emulsion from the areas not exposed to the light.

WASHING OUT

Being able to wash your screen out with a powerful shower head attachment is an important aspect of screen printing. To wash out a screen after it has been exposed, firstly wet it on both sides with a jet of cold water. With the frame side facing you, begin to fully drench it with the strongest jet of water you have. After working slowly across the image, you should be able to see a faint outline of it on the screen. The water jet will begin to wash away the non-exposed 'black' areas of the image. Keep working the jet around the screen until the whole of the image is fully revealed. If you are having any difficulties, try flipping the screen over and jet washing any stubborn bits from the other side. If the image does not 'wash out' you may have over-exposed your screen; if it all washes away, you may have under-exposed it. Either way, you will need to reconsider your exposure time and start again.

You may also need to wash the screen in between colours as well as at the end of the project. It is economical and less messy if you begin by scooping up any excess ink in the frame with a squeegee and returning it to the mixing cup before you wash the screen. In a home environment you can put the frame in a bath or shower and rinse it off thoroughly. As the inks used here are water-based they will not stain your bath and should be easy to remove from the screen, providing you keep the screen active and you do not let them dry on the mesh.

BABY OIL STENCILS

Use a brush or sponge to coat photocopies with a small amount of baby oil to ensure even coverage. This will make them transparent, and you can double up photocopied images to create a stronger image for exposure. Once the photocopies are covered in the oil it should be easy to slide them together and register them. Use a window or light box to help you.

REMOVING STENCILS

Paper stencils can be removed readily from a screen and discarded. However, photographic emulsion, drawing fluid and brown screen filler (used in the Fiesta Invitations project on page 94), and oil pastel (used in the Out of this World Cushion project on page 86) all need to be removed with special screen cleaners. The drawing fluid and brown filler come with their own screen cleaner, which is painted onto the screen prior to washing out. Detailed instructions come with the cleaner and should be followed carefully. White spirit is needed to dissolve oil pastel from the mesh, before blasting it with a shower of water, so this should be done outdoors or in a well-ventilated area with appropriate care taken.

All photographic emulsions have their own proprietary removers, which should be purchased at the same time as the emulsion. Similar to the filler, the emulsion remover is brushed onto the screen to encourage the emulsion to dissolve before washing out. Read all manufacturer's instructions carefully for specific details.

14. Colour Blur Placemats

If you love colour, being expressive with paint and are happy to play a game of chance, then this technique is for you. Requiring limited materials, these placemats can easily be made in an afternoon. Colour blur is essentially a monoprint technique, allowing you to create one-of-a-kind painterly prints while exploring multiple colour blends. Expressive, quick and fun, this project shows you how to create a dining set that won't look like anyone else's!

Materials and tools

Stencil paper or
  baking parchment
4 cork placemats
Pencil
Craft knife
Cutting mat
Brown parcel tape
Masking tape
Silk screen
Acrylic paints in several
  different colours
Textile printing medium
Mixing containers and spoons
Squeegee
Greaseproof paper
Iron
Varnish or wax
4 cork coasters (optional)

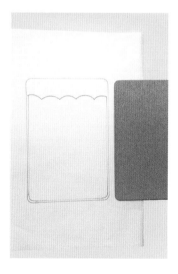

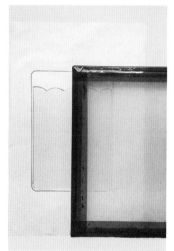

1.

Cut a piece of stencil paper to fit your screen, then place your mat in the centre and draw around it with a pencil. Design a simple shape that will allow you to experiment with blending colour. Make the shape at least 5 mm (¼ in) smaller than the mat on all sides.

2.

Cut out your shape with a craft knife on a cutting mat, and discard the inner piece. Repeat steps 1 and 2 to create four paper stencils, one for each mat. Use parcel tape to cover the outer 2 cm (¾ in) of your screen edges. This will create a well for your ink to sit in. Attach the stencil to the mesh side of the screen, securing it with masking tape.

3.

Mix your printing inks using acrylic paint and textile printing medium according to the instructions on the printing medium (usually a ratio of 1:1). Place the screen on top of the placemat, with the mesh side of the screen down. You should be able to feel the edges of the mat through the mesh to 'register' it in the correct position.

HANDY TIP
There are many different designs you can try out when applying the printing ink to your screen, so it is worth experimenting on paper before you print on your mats.

4.

Blob your colours freely across the open space on the screen, ensuring there is ink at the top of the design.

5.

Holding the screen in place with your free hand, dip your squeegee into the ink at the top of the design and pull the blobbed ink through the screen. Pass the ink backwards and forwards across your design – two or three times should be enough to get good coverage of the placemat without blending the colours too much.

6.

As you pass the squeegee through, the colours will blend further. To keep your colours fresh, repeat the process for each placemat, washing the screen at the end of each print and waiting for it to dry. You will need a new stencil for each print.

7.

When each design is dry, iron it with a medium-to-hot iron, placing greaseproof paper between the iron and the placemat to heat-set it. Protect your unique, printed mats by applying a coat of varnish or a layer of wax on top of the design. You could repeat this process to create a set of matching coasters.

15. Strike a Pose Scarf

Screen printing with paper stencils can be incredibly effective, and the complexity of the designs you print depends entirely on your skill with a craft knife. Inspired in part by the late great fashion icon Isabella Blow and the popular Victorian craft of silhouette cutting, this project focuses on the repetition of the silhouette as a design motif. The silhouette emphasises the outline and is often used in fashion terms to describe clothing and body shapes. This project is a perfect way to start your journey in stencil cutting and a fitting homage to those fearless fashionistas who paved the way to make our world a more colourful one in which to live.

Materials and tools

Scissors
Paper, larger than the screen
All-purpose glue
Stencil paper or
  baking parchment
Pencil
Craft knife
Cutting mat
Masking tape
Silk screen
Brown parcel tape
Plain cotton or wool scarf
Bulldog clips (optional)
Acrylic paint
Textile printing medium
Mixing container and spoon
Squeegee
Iron

1.

On a large piece of paper arrange the cut-out silhouettes from the photocopied templates (pages 78–9) into a layout you would like to repeat print across your scarf. This will be the template for your stencils and must fit on your silk screen with a good border around it. You could draw around your screen first on the paper as a guide. If your screen is small you may need to make two stencils, dividing the silhouettes between them. When you are satisfied with your arrangement, glue the silhouettes in place.

2.

Lay a large piece of stencil paper over the template you have just made and trace the images with a pencil. Stencil paper is relatively thin so you should be able to see the images through it. If not, put your template up against a window so that the light shines through. Trace the silhouettes. Make two stencils.

3.

Lay your traced stencils on a cutting mat and cut out the silhouettes carefully with a craft knife.

4.

Use masking tape to attach one of the stencils to the mesh side of your screen.

5.

Turn your frame over and
create a border around the
edge with brown parcel tape,
to secure your stencil further
and to plug any gaps the
stencil has not blocked
out fully.

6.

Lay your scarf flat on your
table and secure the edges
with tape or bulldog clips. Mix
your paint and printing
medium together according
to the medium's instructions
(usually a ratio of 1:1). Make
enough ink to print the whole
scarf. Place your screen at the
top left-hand corner of your
scarf to begin with.

7.

Print your first screen. My
squeegee isn't big enough
for the image size so I used
two pulls to flood the screen.
Make three passes of ink
across your screen.

8.

You now have your first print on the scarf. As this print is still wet, when you decide where to put your next print make sure your screen is not in contact with it. You will need to work quite quickly before the screen blocks. As my scarf is very long I was able to carry on printing by pulling more of it along the table as I went along. When you have printed all the areas you can for now, scoop out any excess ink, get rid of your stencil and use a shower head attachment to wash out your screen.

9.

Both your screen and the scarf need to dry completely before you can go back to fill the spaces you couldn't print previously. You can speed up the drying time by using a hairdryer on the printed areas. Filling in gaps takes a bit of preparation. Put a new stencil on the dry screen, and lay your screen mesh side down in the space you want to fill. Without ink on the screen you will be able to see previous prints through the mesh. Arrange your screen to avoid those prints. If you can see a silhouette print through one of your stencil cut-outs you will need to block it off with paper and masking tape so that you avoid printing on top of another shape.

10.

Your silhouettes will stand out if the scarf isn't too busy. When you are satisfied, let the scarf dry flat (again, you can speed up the process with a hairdryer). Iron with a medium-to-hot iron on the reverse side, applying pressure for a few minutes on the reverse of each print. This will heat-set your inks, making them stable for laundry purposes.

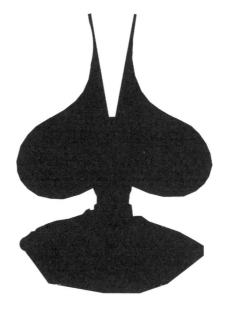

16. Papercut Bunting

The craft of paper stencil cutting is a gratifying way to make print imagery. Taking its inspiration from traditional Mexican 'papel picado' banners, with their intricately cut designs, this project is printed from three paper stencils. If you can develop good knife-cutting skills the prints you produce can become increasingly detailed, although what I enjoy most about this style is its unassuming naivety. This is not a project to be rushed, as the layers of colours need to dry completely before being overprinted, so take your time and the results will not disappoint.

Materials and tools

3 sheets of stencil paper
  or baking parchment
Pencil
Permanent marker
Cutting mat
Craft knife
Scissors
Silk screen
Masking tape
Brown parcel tape
8-10 rice paper sheets
Acrylic paint in 3 colours
Screen printing medium
3 mixing containers and spoons
Squeegee
Stapler
String

1.

Use a pencil to trace a photocopy of each template from pages 84–5 onto the middle of a sheet of stencil paper. Each sheet should be large enough to cover your screen. Define the designs with a marker. Each colour requires a separate stencil – in this case we are printing in black, orange and neon green.

2.

Place your main design on a cutting mat and use a craft knife to cut out the intricate paper stencil carefully on a cutting mat. Take your time as this layer is the most important one, and any mistakes made here may affect the overall design.

3.

Cut out the orange and green layer stencils. In comparison to the black layer these stencils should be quite straightforward to cut out.

4.

Lay the black layer stencil on your table, ensuring it is the right way up. Place your screen on top, mesh side down. Mark around the edge and cut the stencil to size. With the mesh side of the screen facing up, lay the stencil on top and secure it to the frame with masking tape. Turn the frame over and use brown parcel tape to make a border around the inside edge to mask off any gaps and prevent unwanted ink escaping onto your design. In the next steps, you will have to work quickly before the ink dries on the surface of your screen, so make sure you have all you need to hand and that the rice paper is cut to a slightly bigger size than the design before you begin.

5.

Use masking tape to secure your first piece of rice paper to your work surface. Mix your printing ink using black acrylic paint and printing medium according to the instructions (usually a ratio of 1:1). Load up the screen with the ink and print. Two consistent pulls of your printing ink with the squeegee will be sufficient for good coverage.

6.

Rice paper is strong; no ink should transfer to your table. Peel back your screen to reveal your first printed layer. Hang this first print to dry and repeat this process to make multiple pieces for your bunting. Remove and discard your stencil and wash out your screen with a shower head attachment. Allow to dry.

7.

When the first prints are dry, tape one to your print surface. Attach the orange layer stencil to your screen and place it over the taped-down first print so that it lines up. Cut small pieces of parcel tape to cover the mouths of the skulls and apply them to the mesh side of the screen. The tape is useful for blocking off intricate areas.

To make multiple prints you need to be efficient – be sure to prepare everything in advance. Depending on your space, you could line up more than one print at a time. If your screen becomes blocked midway through printing and you need to wash it out, cut another stencil while it dries.

8.

Mix your second colour with a little more print medium in it – at a ratio of 1:2 – and print over the black layer. Again, two pulls of colour will be sufficient. Repeat this process on the remaining prints. Discard your spent stencil and wash the screen again. Allow the prints and the screen to dry.

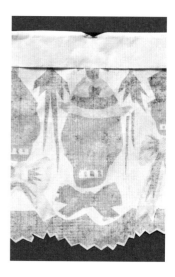

9.

The final layer is the neon green one. Attach the green layer stencil to the dry screen and line it up over the top of your first taped-down print. Refer to the master design on page 81 if you are unsure of the correct positioning. Mix the green to the same 1:2 ratio as the orange, and overprint on your orange-and-black design.

10.

Repeat to print the last colour on each piece of rice paper. Initially some of the black detail will be obscured on your prints, but as the orange and green printing ink dry they will become more transparent. Put all the finished prints to one side to dry.

11.

When the prints are dry, cut around them, following the decorative edging. Leave enough edging at the top of the print to be folded over and stapled to a piece of string. Line up and attach your prints to the string to finish your spooky Halloween bunting.

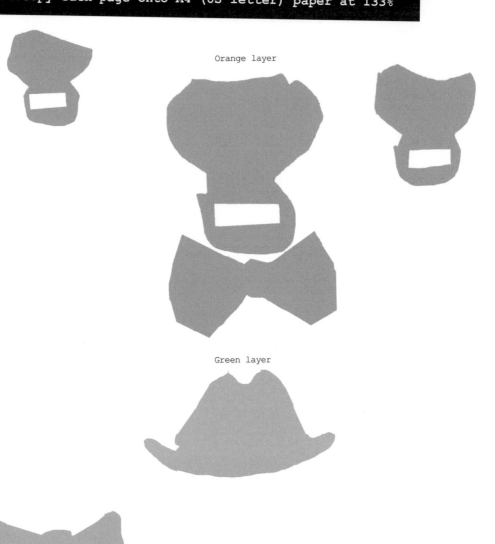

Orange layer

Green layer

Top

17. Out of this World Cushion

Frottage is a surrealist art technique that uses rubbings from textured surfaces to create imagery. This 'low-fi' method of printmaking allows you to make rubbings of textures that catch your eye directly onto your screen. The printing process needs very few items of equipment to be successful. It does take some practice, but it is fascinating to see which textures will translate best when rubbed directly onto the screen mesh. This simple project will excite those with an eye for texture and surface pattern.

Materials and tools

Plain cushion cover and pad
Thin card to fit cushion cover
Stencil paper or baking parchment
Pencil
Craft knife
Cutting mat
Silk screen
Masking tape
Brown parcel tape
Acrylic paint in 2 colours
Textile printing medium
2 mixing containers and spoons
Squeegee
Oil pastel in a light colour
Different textures
Ruler
White spirit
Wide paintbrush
Cotton bud
Greaseproof paper
Iron

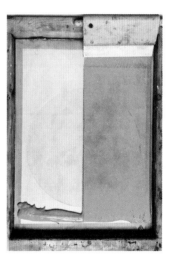

1.

Insert a piece of card inside the cushion cover to stop ink leaking through. Cut two pieces of stencil paper slightly bigger than your print screen. Use a pencil to draw round a dinner plate on both pieces to create a circle to fit your cushion. Set one aside, and cut one out with a craft knife on a cutting mat.

2.

Use masking tape to secure the cut stencil to the frame of your screen on the mesh side, ensuring that there are no gaps around the edges. Use brown parcel tape to create a border around your screen on the frame side, to make a well for your ink.

3.

Line the screen up on top of your cover, feeling the edges through the screen to centre the circle. Mix your printing ink using acrylic paint and textile printing medium according to the instructions (usually a ratio of 1:1). Pull your colour through the screen three times to leave a circular print on the fabric.

4.

Discard the used paper
stencil and wash your screen.
Both the screen and the cover
need to be dry before you
progress to the next stage.
You can speed up this process
with a hairdryer.

5.

With your clean and
dry screen have fun
experimenting with different
texture rubbings. Place your
screen over the texture, mesh
side down, and hold it firmly
in place. With a light-coloured
oil pastel, scribble or rub
directly onto the mesh
of the screen to reveal
a frottage impression.

6.

Try different found textures.
However, be careful not to
select anything that could rip
or puncture the screen's mesh.
Alongside the rubbings, try
expressing yourself further by
mark-making and drawing
directly onto the screen.

7.

When you have a selection
of impressions that you are
happy with, you can cut your
second stencil. With a pencil
and ruler, divide the circle into
eight 'pie' pieces. With a craft
knife, cut all of the circle away
leaving one slice of the 'pie'
on the cutting mat. Attach
the paper stencil to the
screen as before.

8.

Register the screen on top of the block circle you have already printed. You should be able to see the circle clearly enough through the screen.

HANDY TIP
Rather than using white spirit to remove oil pastel from the screen when you have finished printing you could source an eco-friendly alternative from a larger art store or online.

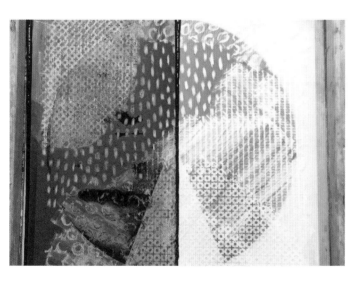

9.

Mix acrylic paint and textile printing medium to form a contrasting ink colour, and print your new stencil with the frottage textures on top of the block colour. Pass the ink through the screen three times. Remove the paper stencil and wash out the screen. The oil pastel will not wash out with water alone. When you have removed all of the printing ink, outdoors or in a well-ventilated area away from any open flames, apply a liberal amount of white spirit to the mesh of the screen with a wide paintbrush, working it into the oil pastel. The pastel should begin to melt away. Repeat until all of the pastel has been removed. Rinse the screen thoroughly with water.

10.

Allow the design to dry. Some of the oil pastel may have transferred through the mesh of the screen. You can remove this when the design is dry with a cotton bud and small amount of white spirit. Heat-set your design by ironing it with a hot iron, but use greaseproof paper to protect the new print. Insert a cushion pad.

18. Into the Woods Wall Frieze

This magical children's wall frieze combines cut-out silhouettes of woodland critters with real foliage to make a repeat pattern on a roll. This technique demonstrates how to use found ephemera and cut-out shapes as masks with photographic emulsion. Into the Woods celebrates the work of the pioneering filmmaker Lotte Reiniger. Create your own dark fairytale with the playful manipulation of found materials and a fertile imagination.

Materials and tools

Roll of wallpaper or
  lining paper
Pencil
Long ruler
Craft knife
Cutting mat
Cut-out shapes
Leaves, flowers and ephemera
Silk screen
Photographic emulsion
Clear acrylic or glass sheet,
  to fit screen
Exposure unit
Brown parcel tape
Bulldog clip
Acrylic paint
Printing medium
Mixing container and spoon
Squeegee
A3 (US tabloid) printer paper

1.

Decide on the height of your frieze. Make sure it is less than half of the shortest side of your silk screen. Measure and mark this distance at regular intervals along one edge of the paper roll. Use a long ruler or straight edge to draw a line parallel to the edge. With a cutting mat underneath, cut along the marked line with a craft knife, using the ruler as a guide.

2.

You will have to print your frieze in sections according to the length of your screen. To help you repeat your design along the length of the frieze, cut two sections of paper from the end of your frieze roll, each of which should fit three quarters of the length of your screen. Use these as templates to plan your frieze design in two parts. Using small leaves, flowers and paper cut-outs, lay out a different design on each piece of paper. Leave a small gap at each end of your paper templates to make it easier to repeat the pattern along your frieze. Don't stick the elements down to the pieces of paper – just use the space to experiment until you are happy with your arrangements.

3.

Coat your screen with photographic emulsion and place it in a dark space to dry (see pages 66–7). When dry, transfer the leaves and cut-outs from your templates to your coated screen, mesh side up, keeping the pieces within the dimensions of your paper templates.

4.

Place a large piece of clear glass or acrylic over your design to help weigh it down. Expose your screen for about 20 minutes (see pages 67–8). You may need to experiment with this timing depending on your set-up and lamp strength.

Wash out the image using a shower head attachment with cold water. Allow the screen to dry. Tape around the edge of your designs on the frame side to create a well for your ink and to aid the registration of the repeat pattern. Tape carefully along the edges, keeping straight lines.

5.

Secure the roll of frieze paper to your print table at one end with a bulldog clip or tape and, using a long ruler or measuring tape, mark out the length of your pattern templates all the way along your roll on the table. Draw a pencil line across the width of your paper at these interval marks; you will use these lines to help guide you as you repeat your design along the roll. Block out one of the designs by taping paper over it on the mesh side, so that you don't print it by mistake.

Line up your screen with the edge of the length of paper. Your brown tape line should help you keep the design straight. Mix your printing ink using acrylic paint and printing medium according to the instructions on the printing medium (usually a ratio of 1:1) and load up the screen with this mix.

HANDY TIP
Make sure you mix plenty of your printing ink and keep it in a sealed container. It is very difficult to go back and colour-match later if you run out of ink.

7.

Use your second exposed design to go back to the gaps and repeat the same process. It can be tricky to see the pencil lines, so use a piece of A3 (US tabloid) white printer paper as a guide along the edge of the first design to help you see where to join your image. Take your time.

6.

Hold your screen down firmly and pull your ink across the screen twice.

While your first design is active, repeat the printing process along the length of the roll on the table at every other interval according to your pencilled lines. You are leaving gaps that you will go back and fill in with your second design. You can speed up the drying time by using a hairdryer.

HANDY TIP
Flood your screen to keep it active for longer (see page 66), or wash it at regular intervals if it is getting blocked.

19. Fiesta Invitations

Making your own party invitations is the perfect way to personalise your special event. Using screen drawing fluid replicates the painted line on a page, and your lines can be bold, organic or intricate just like brushmarks on paper. The viscosity of the fluid is different from paint, but with a bit of practice, drawing directly onto your screen will enable you to reproduce your design over and over, although each one will feel special and handmade. This method has a few stages that require patience, but you will be rewarded if you stick at it. The resulting screen is extremely stable and will work for hundreds of prints, providing you don't allow the ink to dry in the mesh.

Materials and tools

Thin paper
Permanent marker
Silk screen
Screen drawing fluid
Container
Paintbrush
Screen filler
Squeegee
Brown parcel tape
Scissors
Masking tape
Coloured card, slightly larger
  than your design
Acrylic paint
Printing medium
Mixing container and spoon
Envelopes

1.

Using thin paper such as printer paper, trace the template from page 97 or draw your own design with a permanent marker. As the paper is thin, the marker should bleed through to the other side.

2.

Pour a little drawing fluid into a container. If it is too thick it will create a blobbed line. Aim for the consistency of single cream. Add a little water if it is too thick and stir well. Flip the paper over and, with the screen frame side down, use a paintbrush to trace the image through mesh of the screen with the drawing fluid. Allow the image to dry flat.

3.

The blue drawing fluid will wash out of the screen in step 4 to become the printed line and the brown filler will block the screen. Hold the screen with one hand and squeegee the filler onto the mesh side with the other. Do this in one pull, maintaining firm, even pressure. Multiple pulls dissolve the drawing fluid and ruin the image.

4.

When dry, use a shower head attachment to wash the drawing fluid out of the screen with cold water. Use a little warm water to remove any stubborn areas of drawing fluid. Surround the image with a border of brown parcel tape to contain the printing ink and stop the ink flooding onto your card or table.

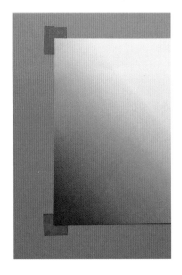

5.

On your work surface mark out where your card will sit with masking tape. In this instance I am using an A4 (US letter) colour-gradient craft card.

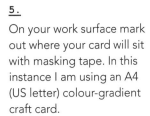

HANDY TIP
If your screen starts to block as the ink dries, resulting in your image not printing sharply, wash your screen out using a shower head attachment. Once it has dried you can start printing again.

6.

Line up your screen to fit the card, making sure the image fits onto it. To ensure you line your screen up to the same position each time, mark up the screen position with tape too. It makes life much easier if you do this now as once the screen is covered in ink, it will become difficult to see the card beneath.

7.

Mix your printing ink using acrylic paint and acrylic printing medium according to the instructions (usually a ratio of 1:1). Run a line of ink along one side of the design.

8.

Holding the screen in place, pull the ink across your image with a squeegee. Tap the ink out at the other side and make a second pull back. Put your printed fiesta invite to one side and reload your paper using the guide marks. Replenish your ink and print again. Your design should register up as the original did each time.

TEMPLATE
Photocopy onto A3 (US tabloid) paper at 150%

9.

Stick to one colour or wash your screen out thoroughly, leave it to dry and get into the party spirit by experimenting with other colours. Let your prints dry fully before trimming them to size. Fold and write the invitations.

20. Doodlebug Napkins

In this project, you will doodle directly onto your silk screen and print with expandable puff binder onto napkins. This is such an impressive print technique, and I never get tired of the moment you watch your designs puff up and spring into life. It may take a little practice, but once you get the hang of it you can impress your guests with these textured 3D designs.

Materials and tools

Silk screen
Drawing fluid
Mixing container and spoon
Paintbrush
Screen filler
Squeegee
Brown parcel tape
Scrap paper
Acrylic paint
Expandable puff binder
  for textiles
Plain fabric napkins
Baking parchment
Iron

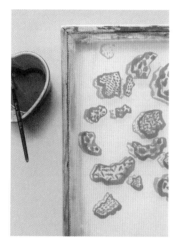

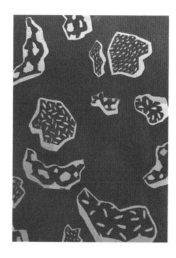

1.

Lay your silk screen frame side down on your print table. Stir your drawing fluid and decant a little into a container. Add a little water if it is too thick and stir well to achieve the consistency of single cream. With a paintbrush, doodle directly onto your screen with the drawing fluid, or use a drawing underneath as a guide.

2.

When the fluid is dry, use a squeegee to cover your screen with one even coat of screen filler on the mesh side. This can be tricky as you need to get the filler coat right first time. Several attempts can cause the blue drawing fluid to dissolve. One even coat with good pressure is key here. Keep the screen flat and let the filler coat dry.

3.

When the screen is dry, wash out the drawing fluid with a shower head attachment using cold water. Add a little warm water to remove any stubborn bits. Put the screen somewhere safe to dry. Once dry, use brown parcel tape to cover the edges of the screen where any filler did not reach. If your screen is fully coated you do not need to do this.

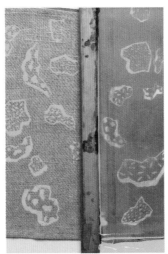

4.

Place one of your napkins on your work surface. As the napkins are relatively small, you don't need to secure them to the table. Place some scrap paper underneath your napkin to protect your table.

5.

Mix your acrylic paint with the expandable puff binder according to the puff binder packet instructions (usually the ratio is 1:1). Holding the screen with one hand and the squeegee with another, pull the printing ink three times across the entire image. Try to ensure even coverage each time. Hold the edge of the napkin down as you lift the screen away.

6.

Leave the napkin to dry (you can speed this up with a hairdryer). Depending on the size of your screen, you may need to print another section of your napkin if it is not fully covered with the first print. Refresh the scrap paper on your work surface before you do this. Repeat this process for all of your napkins. You will need to work quickly so that your screen doesn't block.

7.

When your prints are completely dry, protect your ironing board with some baking parchment and iron the napkins on the reverse with a hot iron. Then the magic happens – the heat will cause the ink to puff up to form tactile 3D designs.

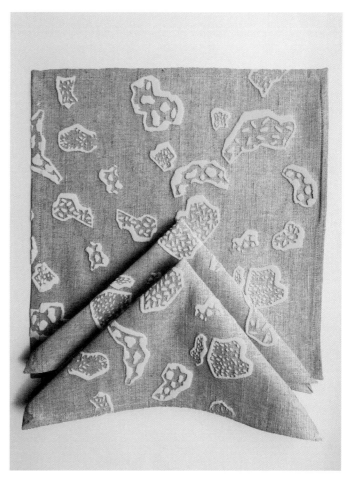

21. Say Yes! T-shirt

Print your own slogan T-shirt in this two-stage screen printing project. You will explore colour blends and add dimension to your slogan with expandable puff binder to create a raised surface. Colour blends, half-drop shadow and spongy text – what is not to love about that? Use your T-shirt to express yourself. Got something on your mind? What do you want to say?

Materials and tools

Paper
Pencil
Permanent marker pen
Silk screen
Thin piece of card
Drawing fluid
Paintbrush
Brown parcel tape
Screen filler
Scissors
Squeegee
Plain T-shirt
Acrylic paint
Textile printing medium
Mixing containers and spoons
Iron
Craft knife
Cutting mat
Expandable puff binder

1.

Prepare the slogan you want to print on your T-shirt. You may decide to draw your slogan freehand, or, as I have done, use a universal computer font and print it out. Arrange your words as you want them to appear on the printed T-shirt. It's a good idea to use a bold font for this as you want your text to be seen.

2.

Use a pencil to trace the slogan onto another piece of paper to keep the 'master' copy clean in case you need it again. Define the slogan with a permanent marker pen.

3.

Place the drawing under your screen to trace from, and prop the screen slightly away from the table with a thin piece of card. The screen needs to be frame side up and mesh side down.

4.

Use a paintbrush to trace the outline of the letters carefully with the drawing fluid, and fill in the whole of their shapes. Place the screen somewhere flat to dry. When dry, surround the text with a border of brown parcel tape, leaving just a small border around the text.

5.

Flip your screen over so that the screen frame is on the print table and the mesh side is facing you. Your text will appear back to front. Apply a small amount of the screen filler to the top of your image, being mindful to stay within the brown tape. In one firm pull with your squeegee, cover the area inside the tape border with filler.

6.

Carefully scoop off any excess filler with your squeegee or a damp sponge. Allow to dry, keeping the screen flat to prevent the filler from dripping. When completely dry, use a shower head attachment to wash the blue drawing fluid out from the screen. Again, allow the screen to dry before moving on to printing.

HANDY TIP
If you would like to print multiple T-shirts, repeat steps 7-8 on each one before you move on to steps 9-13.

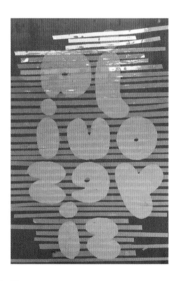

7.

Insert a large piece of thin card inside the T-shirt. Place your screen mesh side down onto your T-shirt and make adjustments to line it up centrally by feeling the edges of your T-shirt through the screen. Mix your first colour. Holding your screen down with one hand, pull the colour through your image. Make a second and then a third pull.

8.

Scoop up any excess ink on your screen and return it to the mixing container. Wash out your screen thoroughly and set it aside to dry. When your text is completely dry, turn the T-shirt inside out and use a hot iron to heat-set the ink permanently.

9.

Use a craft knife and cutting mat to prepare thin strips of brown tape to use as a mask over the text. Arrange the tape in a regular formation on the mesh side of your screen directly on top of the text. Mix up your overprint colours (I have used two), combining them with the puff binder.

10.

Line up the screen on top of your text. You should be able to see your first print through the mesh. Move the screen slightly out of alignment.

To achieve a horizontal colour blend, apply your colours in a variegated line along the length of the text.

11.

Holding the screen in place with one hand, pull the colours from left to right across the screen. Pull again from right to left, lining up the squeegee to match the colours. Pull one more time if there is enough ink and if the colours have not become too mixed. Use the other side of the squeegee if you need to.

12.

Your revealed print will be an offset colour blend of stripes and will initially look like a regular flat screen print. Allow the print to dry naturally or speed the drying time with a hairdryer. Once completely dry, turn the T-shirt inside out and insert a piece of card to prevent it sticking to itself when you heat-set the print.

13.

Gently run a medium-to-hot iron over the back of the print. As you do so you should see the surface of the T-shirt begin to pucker. When all the puckering has finished, turn the T-shirt the right way around. The striped text will have puffed up from the surface.

22. Retro Tech Pencil Case

Combining different printmaking methods can make imaginative, original designs. This project merges two techniques into one: foiling and colour printing. The design is exposed onto a silk screen using photographic emulsion, enabling the fine detail of the drawings to be translated. Drawing freehand with permanent markers is a liberating experience, as you can produce multiple designs cheaply and spontaneously. As fine line drawings are also quite easy to expose onto a screen with a home exposure kit, this opens up exciting possibilities for designs with a handcrafted aesthetic. Celebrating vintage technology in all its glory, this retro tech pencil case retains the characteristic hand of its maker.

Materials and tools

A4 (US letter) white paper
Pencil
Plain cloth pencil case
Felt tips, various sizes
2 sheets of A4 (US letter) acetate
Permanent marker
Silk screen
Photographic emulsion
Squeegee
Clear acrylic or glass sheet,
  to fit screen
Exposure unit
Brown parcel tape
Masking tape
Acrylic paint
Textile printing medium
Mixing container and spoon
Metallic foil binder
Metallic foil
Baking parchment
Iron

1.

On a piece of white paper, draw around your pencil case with a pencil. Make a linear 'master' drawing of your design using felt tips in different thicknesses to create varying strengths of line. This process uses two different printing mediums, so the design is split in two layers.

2.

Trace the two separate layers within your drawing onto two pieces of acetate with a black permanent marker. My first layer will be printed in a mid- blue and the second in metallic foil.

3.

Flip your acetates over and go over the line drawings on the other side of the acetates with the permanent marker. This will ensure that your design is tonally dark enough to block out the light when exposed and make crisp lines.

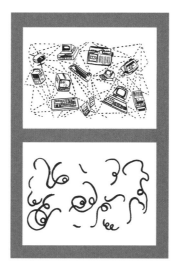

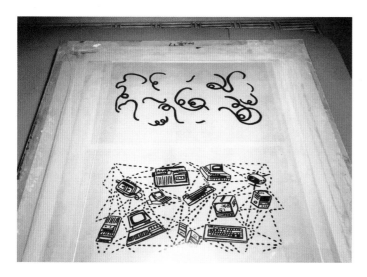

4.

Coat your screen with photographic emulsion and allow it to dry in a dark space. In subdued lighting, lay your screen on the exposure table with the frame side down. Lay the acetates on top of the mesh with the imagery back to front. Weigh the acetates down with a sheet of clear acrylic or glass. Expose the screen – in my example I have done this for 8 minutes (see page 67).

<u>5.</u>

Wash your screen out and use
brown parcel tape around the
images on the frame side to
define the edges and prevent
unwanted ink transferring to
your print surface. This is a
two-print process, with one
print in ink and the other in
foiling glue.

<u>6.</u>

As the pencil case is quite
small, secure it to the reverse
of your exposed screen with
masking tape. Begin with the
more complex design first.

<u>7.</u>

Mix your printing ink using
acrylic paint and textile
printing medium according
to the instructions on the
printing medium (usually
a ratio of 1:1). Then, pass
the ink three times across
your image.

<u>8.</u>

Use a hairdryer to speed up
the drying time, then flip the
pencil case over and print the
other side. Wash your screen
so that the printing ink doesn't
contaminate the next stage.

9.

When your screen and pencil case are dry, line up the second image over the printed pencil case. You should be able to see the print through the mesh of the screen. Pass the foil binder three times through the screen and across the printed pencil case. Return any excess binder to the pot and wash out the screen.

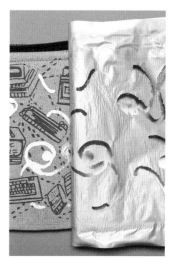

10.

Allow to dry naturally or again speed up the process with a hairdryer until the binder fluid is tacky but not completely dry. Always follow the manufacturer's instructions. Lay a sheet of metallic foil over the surface of the binder and place a piece of baking parchment on top.

11.

Iron with a hot iron, pressing down firmly as you go. Carefully lift up a corner to check whether the foil has stuck. If it has not yet fully adhered, keep ironing for a bit longer.

12.

Peel back the foil carefully to reveal your second layer. The foil will have stuck to the areas where there is binder. Rub your finger over the surface of the lines to get rid of any stray foil. Repeat on the reverse of the pencil case. One final iron over each side using the baking parchment will ensure that the printing ink is heat-set.

TEMPLATES
Photocopy onto A4 (US letter) paper at 100%
or enlarge or shrink to fit your pencil case

TOP

TOP

23. Dada Photomontage Book

This project combines the versatile method of acetone transfer printing with screen printing. In acetone transfer printing, the impression sinks into the paper, and by combining it with screen-printed impressions, you can achieve fascinating results. Inspiration for photomontage can come from anywhere – you could use images from vintage magazines, for example, or any other high-contrast photos. I decided to manipulate and combine the images and apply text to the compositions in a surreal but decorative way. These bespoke books are a tribute to the ground-breaking Dada artists that inspired them, in particular Hannah Höch who was very influential in validating photomontage, enabling it to become a respected artistic practice.

Materials and tools

Scrap paper
Heavyweight cartridge paper
Ruler
Pencil
Scissors
Old magazines for photo
 and typography cuttings
Masking tape
Acetone
Non-plastic container
Paintbrush
Silk screen
Photographic emulsion
Squeegee
Baby oil
Brush or sponge
Exposure unit
Brown parcel tape
Acrylic paint
Printing medium
Scrap paper for blotting
Stencil/printer paper for
 masking screen
Mount card, 14 × 10 cm (5^1/$_2$ × 4 in)
Plain cotton fabric, 30 cm (12 in) square
Spray glue
Double-sided tape or all-purpose glue

BOOK PATTERN 1

20 x 56 cm
 (8 × 22 in)
8 boxes 10 × 14 cm
 (4 × 5^1/$_2$ in)

BOOK PATTERN 2

14 × 80 cm
 (5^1/$_2$ × 32 in)
8 boxes 10 × 14 cm
 (4 x 5^1/$_2$ in)

1.

Plan your book by cutting out your cartridge paper to the dimensions of your chosen pattern. Pattern 1 has an unusual folding configuration, while pattern 2 is a simple concertina layout. Try out the different folds on scrap paper before you begin to help you plan your compositions.

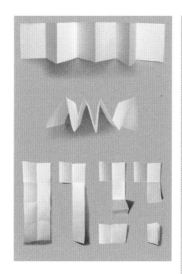

3.

Cut and lay out your copies to make a composition on the first page. Your photocopies should not be more than three days old. Make the folds before printing to help guide your layout decisions. Use masking tape to secure your first photocopy face down. Pour a small amount of acetone into a non-plastic container. Always use acetone outside or in a well-ventilated space away from any open flames, and wear goggles and disposable gloves. With a paintbrush, apply the acetone sparingly to the photocopy. Scribble on the back with a pencil and peel away the paper to reveal the print.

2.

Get creative by cutting out faces from magazines and 'photomontaging' them together. Customise your designs by drawing on top of the images, cutting into them and rearranging them. Find typography that you like from old books and magazines or from unusual fonts found online. Put them together in arrangements separate from the imagery. The typography does not have to say anything, as we are using it solely as a decorative device. Photocopy your collages.

HANDY TIP
Sometimes less is more; don't overcomplicate your designs. Allow some empty space for the design to breathe.

4.

Continue to populate your book pages with imagery. Add text in the same way if you wish, but remember that it will come out in reverse if not flipped horizontally on a photocopier or computer first. Don't use all your text photocopies up; keep some typography back to overprint with. Once you are happy with your acetone prints, move on to screen printing.

HANDY TIP
Look up alternative book-folding ideas online — there are many unusual options to explore and try out. Always do a practice run with scrap paper first to help you plan your page layouts.

5.

Coat your silk screen with photographic emulsion. Lightly cover your photocopies in baby oil to make them translucent. You will need two photocopies of each layout so that you can double them up to create a stronger image. My screen fitted two A3 (US tabloid) layouts so I needed four photocopies. Expose your screen (see pages 67–8). Use brown parcel tape around the edges of the screen on the frame side to create a well for the ink. My layout is close to the edge of the screen which means that my outer text, for example the O, will not print fully. If you don't want your text to be cut off, leave a 3 cm (1¼ in) gap around the edge of your screen.

6.

As acetone dries very quickly you will be able to overprint straight away onto the transfer-printed paper. Decide which element of the exposed screen you want to use and mask off the rest with printer paper and masking tape on the mesh side.

7.

Mix your printing ink using acrylic paint and the paper printing medium according to the instructions on the printing medium (usually a ratio of 1:1). Put scrap paper around your paper to keep your work surface clean. Place your screen in position and print.

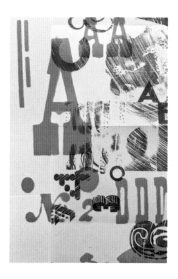

8.

This is the exciting bit – watching your book designs emerge! Blot your screen-printed text with scrap paper before moving around the composition. Unmask your screen to use another part of the design and remask the surrounding areas with fresh paper and masking tape to show only the areas you want to print.

9.

As you unmask your screen you should be able you see through it enough to plan your next print impression. Make sure you don't cover up any previous prints you want to remain bold.

10.

When your book prints are dry, make a front cover. Take the plain cotton fabric and screen print some more of your typography onto it, then blot the print and let it dry thoroughly.

When dry, cut the fabric down to fit your mount card with a border of approximately 2.5 cm (1 in). Cover the back of the printed fabric with spray glue, taking care to lay scrap paper behind the fabric to catch any excess glue. Press the fabric onto the mount card, smoothing out any creases as you go. Fold the excess fabric over to the other side. Use double-sided tape or all-purpose glue to stick the back of the first page to the back of the mount card.

24. Pop! Drawstring Bag

With a nod to Roy Lichtenstein and the pioneers of pop art, this project uses freehand drawing and mark-making to explore typography and line. Halftone dots were used for simulating tone in early newspaper reproduction. Technology has moved on, but you can incorporate this retro device into a design to add depth. The drawings are photographically exposed onto a screen to enable printing in metallic foils. Capable of elevating design ideas into showstoppers, this process promises professional outcomes to the home printmaker.

Materials and tools

Paper, A4 (US letter) size
Permanent marker
2 A4 (US letter) acetate sheets (optional)
Clear tape
Baby oil (if not using acetate)
Brush or sponge (if not using acetate)
Silk screen
Squeegee
Photographic emulsion
Clear acrylic or glass sheet
Exposure unit
Brown parcel tape
Plain drawstring bag
Foil fabric binder
Metallic foils
Baking parchment or greaseproof paper
Iron

1.

Create a pattern, either using the template on page 119 or by making your own line drawings with a permanent marker and combining these with halftone dot-patterns. Halftone dot patterns can be easily found online, downloaded and printed off.

2.

Photocopy your design onto acetate twice, layer the sheets up exactly and tape them together at the edges with clear tape. Alternatively, make two photocopies of your design and lightly cover them in baby oil with a brush or sponge. On a light box or against a window, line up your designs carefully. The baby oil will turn the paper translucent.

3.

In a darkened room, coat your screen with photographic emulsion. Relocate the frame to a completely dark cupboard or space to dry. When it is dry, lay your screen frame side down and place the photocopies on top, reverse side up. Anchor them down with a large piece of glass or clear acrylic. Expose the image for 8 minutes (see pages 67–8).

4.

After exposure, wash out your image with cold water using a shower head attachment and leave the screen to dry.

Use brown parcel tape on the frame side to define the outline of your image and direct your glue layer.

5.

Line up your screen over the drawstring bag, making adjustments to ensure the design is centred. Pull the foil glue through the screen onto the bag, passing it over your image three times to print a white glue image. Wash your screen as soon as possible so the glue does not dry on the mesh.

6.

Wait for the foil glue to become tacky (follow the manufacturer's instructions), or speed this up with a hairdryer. Cut out a selection of different colours from your foils and arrange them over the top of the printed glue areas. Place a piece of baking parchment or greaseproof paper on top and iron with a hot iron. Apply pressure and iron slowly.

7.

Peel up the corners of the foils to take a peek. If the foils have not stuck in parts, replace the parchment paper and continue to apply pressure and heat until the foils are fully stuck down. Peel back the foils carefully to reveal your metallic design. The bag will now be stable enough to use.

25. Punk Apron

Jamie Reid's iconic 1970s punk photomontages changed the face of graphic design forever, inspiring generations of image-makers to come. Channelling the spirit of punk, this project combines photomontage and text to make a screen-printed apron. Use the template provided or create your own designs to print with photo emulsion and a DIY exposure unit. Rough, ready and edgy, this no-nonsense way of direct printmaking makes a bold statement, staying true to the DIY aesthetic from which it originated.

Materials and tools

Silk screen
Photographic emulsion
Squeegee
Baby oil
Brush or sponge
Clear acrylic or glass sheet,
  to fit screen
Exposure unit
Brown parcel tape
Scissors
Plain apron
Black acrylic paint
Textile printing medium
Mixing container and spoon
Newspaper
Iron

1.

Use the template provided on page 123 or create your own design using text and photographs. If you make your own you will need access to a computer or a phone app that will enable you to alter the brightness and contrast of your imagery and to change it into a dotted halftone pattern. You can play around with the contrast of your designs easily on a photocopier, but it will not give you the halftone pattern you need to help you depict the mid-tones of your design. The best designs for this process are ones with high contrast: dark blacks and white whites. When you have finished your pattern, make two photocopies of it.

2.

Coat your screen with photographic emulsion and leave it to dry in a darkened space. While you wait, make the two photocopies of your design translucent by covering them in baby oil with a brush or sponge and line them up exactly on top of each other to strengthen the image. When your screen is fully dry, lay the photocopies on top of it, back to front, weigh them down with a large piece of glass or clear acrylic and expose the image with your exposure unit for 8–15 minutes (see pages 67–8). I exposed my template for 9 minutes. Wash out the screen with cold water using a shower head attachment and wait for it to dry.

3.

Use brown parcel tape to make a border around your design on the frame side to help with registration later on and to create a well for the ink.

4.

Place the plain apron flat on the print table and line up your screen on top, mesh side down. You will be able to see the edges of the apron through the screen to help you plan your first print impression.

5.

Mix your printing ink using acrylic paint and textile printing medium according to the instructions on the printing medium (usually a ratio of 1:1). Apply liberally to the taped area at the top of the screen. Pull the ink through the screen three times, applying pressure.

HANDY TIP
Don't let the ink on your screen dry. Flood your screen between uses if you want to keep it active, or wash it out regularly and let it dry before using again if you have a little more time.

6.

Prints can be affected by any raised areas such as pockets or edging, as they stop the screen from making close contact with the surface of the cloth. In the spirit of the punk aesthetic, however, I'm going to keep these glitches in my design. You may decide to try to print over them again later.

7.

Use a hairdryer to dry your first print. You can then wash your screen out and register your clean screen on top of the first impression with a slight overlap. Alternatively, you could decide to keep your screen active by printing randomly across the apron.

9.

Avoid printing over a wet impression, however. Use a hairdryer to dry the printed area you want to go over or blot the excess ink off with newspaper.

10.

Use a clean screen to correct any mistakes you want to overprint. You should be able to see the printed image through the screen. Assess your apron and decide when you are finished. Using a hot iron, apply pressure to the back of the printed apron. This will heat-set your design so that it can be laundered.

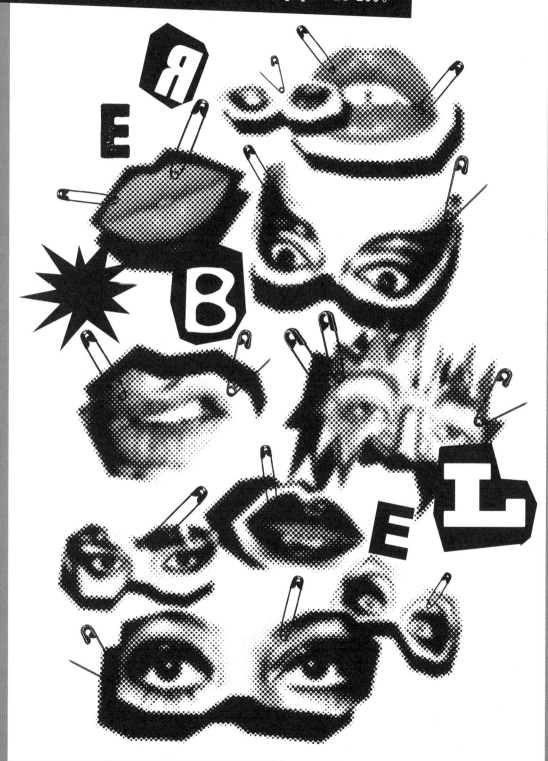

Transfer
Printing

Transfer printing is a loose term I have given to print techniques that fall outside the main disciplines of relief, screen and intaglio (the latter isn't covered here as it requires equipment not readily available to a home printmaker).

We will explore transfer printing with acetone toner prints, cyanotype photography and decal transfers. All of these techniques allow you to transfer imagery to another surface through pressure, heat or light exposure. The methods in this chapter do not require traditional printing inks to make impressions, which makes them ideal processes to practise at home when space is at a premium and you want to avoid the 'mess' of using printing inks.

One of my favourite low-tech print techniques for transferring photographic imagery is acetone transfer, also used in the Dada Photomantage Book project on page 112. This simple process yields impressive, poetic results, with a curious mind and very little equipment being the only requirements. Similarly, cyanotype printing is a great way to enjoy the alchemy of early wet photography, allowing you to connect to this seductive abandoned process and the power of nature.

Decal transfer printing is another technique that takes us back to bygone times. The world of pottery and printmaking have long been closely related; decal transfers were used in the decoration of ceramic wares as early as the seventeenth century. The decal project on page 130 couldn't be simpler and will open up exciting possibilities for decorating items across the whole of your home.

All the projects featured in this chapter will help you rethink what print can be and encourage you to try out these beautifully simple but effective processes.

Transfer Printing Techniques

CYANOTYPE

Cyanotype is the collective name for ferric ammonium citrate and potassium ferricyanide. When the two are mixed together they form an extremely light-sensitive liquid solution. This unstable mixture is notoriously temperamental and cyanotype printing can be difficult to master. On a bright sunny day, a photographic exposure can be made in around 10 minutes, but exposure timings can change radically depending on the cloud cover and time of day. There are lots of online calculators to help you gauge timings for different weather conditions, but you will save time and money if you make test samples. Instructions for mixing the cyanotype solution will come with the product you buy. Only mix up the amount you wish to use as the solution needs to be kept in the dark and only has a short shelf life. All coating of papers or fabrics needs to be done in a darkened room, and the prints must be left to dry flat in complete darkness. A light-secure chest of drawers or cupboard is perfect for this. Once exposed and washed out, the print will change colour over 24 hours before becoming stable. Yellowing can sometimes occur if you do not wash the cyano solution thoroughly from the print after exposure. It is a good idea to replenish the water regularly if you are using a water bath to wash out multiple cyano prints.

HANDY TIP
If you have access to a UV light box this is a great alternative for exposing your prints. Timings will still vary, but it does mean that you can make cyano prints all year round, even when the weather conditions are bad!

DECAL PRINTING

There are a number of customisable print decals on the market. Some need a laminator to stabilise them, some can be set in the microwave and others require a clear varnish after application. I searched for the easiest one to use in this book, requiring the least equipment but yielding stable results. If your budget allows it might be a good idea to test a few different types as they differ in their long-term durability.

HANDY TIP
Some decals may scratch easily if used on plates or regularly washed ceramic ware. Making test samples in advance of your project will enable you to find the best product for your needs.

26. Faded Memories

Laser copy transfer prints are simple, cheap and instantly rewarding. This easy project will demonstrate how to turn your treasured memories and photographs into beautiful vintage-style art prints. This technique was championed in the 1950s by the American artist Robert Rauschenberg, who used this instant printmaking method to transfer and reappropriate found ephemera from magazines and newspapers in his 'Combines'. Mass media printing methods have changed since then, but some magazine prints will still transfer, so have a go!

Materials and tools

Holiday memorabilia
Camera
Acetone
Non-plastic container
Vintage paper
Masking tape
Paintbrush
Pencil

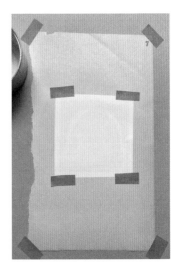

1.

Gather a collection of your favourite holiday memorabilia. Group the items together and take a photograph. Print out the image. Resize your printed image on a photocopier to fit the size of the vintage paper you are using, allowing for a border around the image.

2.

Flip your image if it includes writing, as the transferred image is printed in reverse. Both black-and-white and colour will work, but they must be fresh copies made from a laser printer. Copies more than a couple of days old may not work as the toner hardens and becomes fixed.

3.

Outside or in a well-ventilated space away from open flames and wearing goggles and gloves, pour out a small amount of acetone into a non-plastic container (the acetone can melt plastics). Cut out your laser-copy image and tape it face down to the vintage paper. Secure the vintage paper to the table with tape.

4.

Apply a small amount of acetone to the reverse of the copy with a paintbrush. Try not to 'flood' the image as the toner will bleed and your image will run. Work relatively quickly at this point as the acetone evaporates rapidly.

5.

With a sharp pencil, scribble across the back of the image, applying pressure. Repeat across the copy until the whole of the back of the image has been covered.

6.

Remove the bottom tapes and peel back slowly. If the copy sticks to the paper, apply a bit more acetone to the back of the copy in that area, and scribble over it. This should help to release the toner from the copy and prevent it from sticking. You can also reapply the acetone at this point if there are any sections of the image that you have missed.

7.

This process takes a bit of practice. Try experimenting with your scribble mark-making to achieve different results. Think of exciting ways to display your treasured 'faded memories'. You could mount them in a book or display sleeve, for example.

27. Freestyle Wall Tiles

Decal printing is a great way to upcycle old ceramic tiles. Using colour, pattern and collage offers infinite variations for you to play with, instantly brightening up a tired wall space on a very small budget. Look at Eduardo Paolozzi's spectacular pattern mosaics that he created for the London Underground at Tottenham Court Road station – they are a fabulous source of inspiration. Stick to a restricted colour palette, or colour clash and pattern mash – it's up to you. This interior-design project allows your imagination to run wild.

Materials and tools

Pencil
Paints
Paintbrush
Paper
Scissors
Glue
Ceramic bathroom tiles small
  enough to fit onto A4
  (US letter) paper
Water slide decal papers,
  A4 (US letter) size
Container for water
Small sponge
Cotton fabric or a clean cloth
Rolling pin

1.
Paint or draw a variety of patterns onto scrap pieces of paper. Consider the scale of the marks; if they are too big, they may not fit the tiles.

2.
Cut out shapes from your patterns and experiment with different compositions on the tiles. When you are happy with an arrangement, draw around your tile onto a blank piece of paper and stick your cut-out shapes to the paper.

3.
Photocopy your designs onto decal paper. I have used a laser photocopier, but you can buy different decal papers for inkjet printers. I could fit two designs on one sheet. Cut out each tile design.

4.

Place your decal paper into a container of water big enough for the decal to lie flat. Some decal papers will curl – if yours does, turn it over and soak it for a couple of seconds on the reverse before flipping back.

5.

As your decal becomes saturated, it will begin to release itself from its paper backing. When this starts to happen, carefully remove the decal from the water.

6.

Lay the decal on top of your tile and slide the backing paper away from under it, using a small sponge to hold the decal in place. Avoid touching the decal with your fingers as it is very delicate. Use the sponge to get the decal into position and to smooth out any air bubbles. Work from the centre to the edges to expel air pockets.

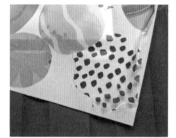

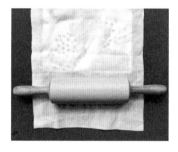
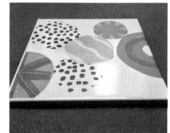

7.

Place cotton fabric or a clean cloth over the top of the decal, and carefully roll a rolling pin across the fabric in all directions. This will release any final air bubbles and blot excess water on the surface. Finally, give your tiles a very gentle polish with the cloth to target any missed bubbles.

8.

Place the tile in the oven at the temperature and time recommended on the decal paper manufacturer's instructions. When you remove your tile from the oven the decal will be fixed to the tile and the edges should be barely visible.

9.

Try placing your decal designs on different coloured tiles to see how the colours interact. Get creative by upcycling your tiles with a riot of colour and pattern.

28. Sunny Day Journal

Cyanotype printmaking is often credited as being one of the earliest forms of photography. It was initially used in the mid-nineteenth century by scientists and engineers to make copies of plans and to document botanical finds. As a direct transfer process, it relies on the sun's light to develop printed imagery. In the 1920s, Man Ray coined the term 'rayograph' to describe his camera-less experiments that used a similar process. Make your own special journal by harnessing the power of the sun.

Materials and tools
Selection of textured objects
2 sheets of clear acrylic
Scissors
Clear sticky tape
Cyano paper
Tray for water
Sketchbook
Spray glue
All-purpose glue
Ribbon

1.

Gather together materials to use as a mask for your cyanotype sun prints. Textures with open weaves or perforations are ideal. Photocopies of textures or patterns on acetate also work well and reveal a surprising amount of detail when you expose your print.

2.

Cut up and arrange your textures onto one of your acrylic sheets, securing them with small pieces of clear sticky tape to keep them in place.

3.

Follow the manufacturer's instructions for your cyano paper. Open the packet and take one sheet out, returning the rest to a dark place.

4.

Sandwich the cyano paper between the two acrylic sheets. One of the sheets will have the textures attached and one will be clear. Using the clear one as a base, place your cyano paper on top of the base with the blue side facing up. Place the sheet with the textures on top. The cyano sheet may be smaller than the sheet of textures so position it to capture the shapes you want to print. Place the assemblage blue side up in direct sunshine to expose it for around 15 minutes. Follow the manufacturer's guidelines.

5.

After exposure to the sun or UV light, your sun print should look like the image above. The masked-off textures will initally look dark.

6.

Place the cyano paper in a bath of cold water and gently move the container to wash the paper. As you wash the print it will change colour and the exposed areas will turn white. Dry flat.

 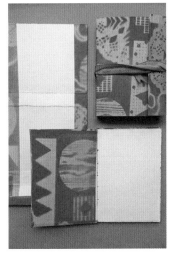 

7.

After 24 hours the sun print will have developed further and its characteristic blue colour will have deepened, as in the photograph above. The paler print on the left is straight from the water bath. The intensified blue print on the right has changed overnight.

8.

Carefully remove the cover of the sketchbook you want to use and either make an exact cardboard replica or repurpose it. Using a light-tack spray glue, back your new cover on both sides with your cyano print. Use an all-purpose glue to secure the spine of your book back in its original position.

9.

Secure the new cover with a contrasting coloured ribbon. You now have a unique journal for imaginative thoughts and extraordinary journeys.

Plate 36
DAMSEL-FLIES—2

29. Photographic Cyano Prints

The alchemy of cyanotype printing brings a sense of magic to this joyful project. The ever-changing colour of the sun print is fascinating to witness as it exposes and develops over a long period of time. The process itself couldn't be simpler, with no tricks or fancy equipment required, just the sun's own rays. Develop your own photographic cyano prints at home to marvel at and enjoy.

Materials and tools

Cyanotype sensitiser kit
Heavyweight cartridge
  or watercolour paper
Foam brush
Acetate sheets
Drawing board
Clear acrylic sheet
Bulldog clip
Tray for water
Watercolour paints
Paintbrush
Green tea (optional)
Decorative gilt tape

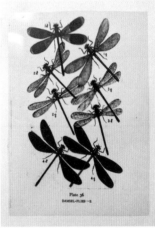

1.

A cyanotype sensitiser kit typically containers the two non-toxic salt compounds potassium ferricyanide and ferric ammonium citrate. When diluted in water and mixed together they form a light-sensitive solution with which you can sensitise your own paper. The kits come with detailed instructions for how to mix them, but typically you need to dilute the salts 24 hours before you wish to apply the solution. When you have mixed and rested your active sensitiser you are ready to apply it. In a darkened room make broad sweeps of the solution across the surface of your paper with a foam brush. Place the coated sensitised paper in a dark cupboard to dry.

2.

Prepare some photographic acetates. This can be done on most laser photocopiers with laser copy acetate sheets. Alternatively, most reprographic print shops can copy an image onto acetate for you. I have used archival encyclopedia images, but many tonal and linear images will work well providing the line or tone is dark enough.

HANDY TIP
If you don't expose your print for long enough it will wash away, too long and it will blur and spoil the image. Avoid frustration by making multiple test samples in advance.

3.

When your papers are dry, lay them sensitised side up on a flat board in a dark space. Place the acetates on top and weigh them down with a piece of clear acrylic. Secure everything in place with a bulldog clip to stop the acetate from moving and to ensure that good contact between the acetate and the coated sensitised paper is maintained.

4.

Here comes the unpredictable part! Take your 'cyano sandwich' outside and place it in direct sunshine. Once in position, be sure not to move it. I exposed my print for 15 minutes on a clear, sunny day, but times will vary depending on weather conditions. After that time, my prints had significantly darkened, and when I removed the acetates the outline of the images I had used was exposed in a shade of light green. It is always worth producing test pieces to work out the optimum exposure times to best suit your image and light quality before you expose your master work.

5.

Bring the sun prints indoors and immerse them in a cold water bath for a few minutes, agitating the water gently to wash out all the remaining solution from the print.

6.

The print colour will change again as you wash it out. The overall appearance will lighten and the exposed areas will wash out white or light blue. The print surface is still developing at this stage and will not be stable for about 24 hours. Over this period the Prussian blue colour will deepen further.

7.

You may decide to keep your cyano prints as they are, or you can experiment with hand-colouring and toning techniques. To change the tone of your cyanotype from blue to dark brown or dark purple, brew a strong jug of green tea. Immerse your cyano print in the tea for about 30 minutes or more, depending on the shade of brown you want to develop. Experiment with timings to tone the prints to a shade to suit your taste.

8.

To make a decorative art print, trim the edges and finish with a gilt tape to add a touch of grandeur.

30. Cosmic Lamp

Extend your knowledge of cyanotype image-making
and discover its wonderful potential in this project.
This photographic method allows you to transfer
intricate, fine line drawings onto the surface of
fabric using only the sun's rays. Cyanotype printing
can be done on many different materials, but this
project will focus on its potential to make fabric
sensitive to light, transforming a ready-made
lamp into a night light with your own sun-printed
cosmic geometric drawings.

Materials and tools

Cyanotype fabric or cyanotype
  sensitiser kit and plain cotton
  fabric
Small lamp with plain lampshade
Pencil
A2 (US medium poster) paper
  for pattern
Scissors
Plain white drawing paper, A4
  (US letter) size
Drawing tools such as
  compass, ruler, protractor,
  spiral stencils
Black fineliner or ballpoint pen
Acetate sheets, A4 (US letter)
  size
Clear sticky tape
Clear acrylic or glass sheet,
  to fit screen
Wooden board or card the same
  size as acrylic
Bulldog clips
Tray for water
Spray glue

1.

You can buy ready-coated cyanotype fabric, but you can also make it yourself quite easily by brushing a piece of plain cotton fabric with cyano solution or dipping the fabric into the solution. Cyano-solution kits come with instructions on mixing.

If you are making your own cyanotype fabric, make sure you prepare it in a dimly lit space and leave it to dry in the dark because it becomes extremely light sensitive. Iron your treated fabric if necessary before use, again in a dimly lit room.

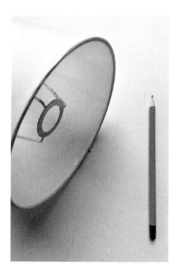

2.

On the A2 (US medium poster) paper, mark out a pattern for your lampshade. Place your lampshade seam side down on the paper and mark the top and bottom. Gently roll your lampshade along its circumference, tracing the path with a pencil on the top and bottom of the lampshade.

3.

Turn the shade a full rotation of the shade until you get back to the seam. Join up the parellel lines to form the flattened shape of your shade. Cut out your paper pattern, allowing for a seam allowance of about 1 cm (⅜ in) all the way around.

4.

Make a series of cosmic geometric drawings onto white paper with a ruler, compass and whatever drawing tools or stencils you have at home. I have used a spiral stencil in some of my examples. Use a black fineliner or ballpoint pen for this.

5.

Photocopy your designs onto A4 (US letter) acetate sheets, making multiple copies so that you can use elements more than once. It is important to make sure the image is tonally dark enough. By doubling up the acetates, your drawn line will be much darker.

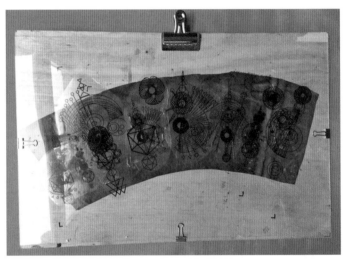

6.

Cut out your cosmic drawings, making sure each one is doubled up and stuck together with clear sticky tape. Arrange the acetates on top of the pattern to make a design you are happy with. Secure them together in that arrangement with clear sticky tape. Be careful not to stick them to the paper pattern.

7.

In a dimly lit room put your paper lampshade pattern on top of the cyano fabric and cut around it. Arrange it on a wooden board into a 'cyano sandwich', with the fabric on top of the board, the cosmic acetates on top of the fabric and a clear acrylic sheet or piece of glass on top of it all. Secure it with bulldog clips to ensure the acetates are in good contact with the fabric. Place in strong sunlight for 15–30 minutes. Weather conditions will affect exposure times, so you may need to experiment. The fabric in my example was exposed for around 20 minutes on a bright sunny day. When you remove the acetates, a white sun-printed impression will be left on the fabric.

8.

Immerse the fabric in cold water and rinse thoroughly to stabilise the print and remove any excess cyano solution.

9.

When the fabric is dry, spray the reverse with spray glue, wait until tacky, then line up and roll your lampshade along the curve of the fabric, smoothing out any air bubbles as you go.

10.

Tuck in the top and bottom edges along their circumferences. Double over the seams and secure them to the reverse side of the shade to give it a professional finish.

11.

Your cosmic lamp is now ready to use. Rather magically, cyano takes 24 hours to fully develop so it may be a tone darker when you wake up in the morning!

Acknowledgements

I would like to thank the cast of many who helped, inspired and supported me to make my first book. Family past and present, and good friends – you know who you are. The incredible team at Octopus who believed in the project enough to get it off the ground and were patient, professional and wise throughout: Zara, Ellie, Jenny, Ben and the behind-the-scenes team of many talents, I salute you. The diverse range of students from different backgrounds, age groups and cultures I have had the great pleasure of nurturing over my many years of teaching. I want you to know that you have inspired me as much I you, I hope. Thank you to the mostly nameless models who gave up their time to be photographed in this book, including my lovely nephew Sebbie. Next time it's you, Isaac.

Lastly a massive thank you to my enduring partner, Chiz, whose perspective, advice and comfort with hugs saw me over the finish line.

Finally, I dedicate this book to my mum for her boundless generosity and resilience and because I think she'd get a kick out of it the most.